Carlo Gébler's novels include AUGUST IN JULY,
WORK AND PLAY, MALACHY AND HIS
FAMILY and LIFE OF A DRUM. His first work of
non-fiction, DRIVING THROUGH CUBA, was
published in 1988. He lives in Northern Ireland.

CARLO GÉBLER

The Glass Curtain
Inside An Ulster Community

An *Abacus* Book

First published in Great Britain in 1991 by Hamish Hamilton
This edition published in 1992 by Abacus

A CIP catalogue record for this book
is available from the British Library.

ISBN 0 349 10338 0

Printed in England by Clays Ltd, St Ives plc

Abacus
A Division of
Little, Brown and Company (UK) Limited
165 Great Dover Street
London SE1 4YA

To Pierre Hodgson

Contents

Acknowledgements

Some of the material in this book has appeared in a different form in *Harpers & Queen* and *Image* magazine. The author gratefully acknowledges the financial assistance of An Chomhairle Ealaíon/The Irish Arts Council.

I would like to thank the following for their help and co-operation: the Army Information Services, particularly Chief Information Officer G. S. Reed, Major C. Baxter and Brad Fleming; Brian E. Barton; the Earl of Belmore; Patrick Bogue; the late Baron Brian de Breffni; Rosemary, Viscountess Brookeborough; the Viscount and Viscountess Brookeborough; Gerry Burns; Frank Cahill; Anne and Joan Casey; George Cathcart; the Centre for Research and Documentation and Caitríona Ruane; Colonel Brian Clark, MC, GM; the Committee on the Administration of Justice; Councillor Paul Corrigan; Mick Cox; Dr Maurna Crozier; P. S. Curran; Kathleen Duncan; the indefatigable staff of Enniskillen Public Library; Enniskillen Together; Julian Evans; Desmond Fennell; Councillor Raymond Ferguson; Reggie Ferguson; Ann Finn; the Rev. Ivan Foster; the Rev. Victor Foster; Margaret Gallagher; Jack Gant; Stan Gebler Davies; Edwin and Mahvash Graham; the Green Party; Tommy Hance; Nick Hanna; the staff of the *Impartial Reporter*, editor Denzil McDaniel and reporter Brian Donaldson; the *Irish Post* and editor Brendan Mac Lua; Gordon and Toni Johnson; Councillor Bert and Olive Johnson; Kate Jones; Eugene Kelly; Councillor Davy Kettyles; Jane Killen; John Lampin; Desmond Lang; Helen Lanigan Wood; Jane Leonard; Councillor Jim Lunny; Séamas Mac Annaidh;

ACKNOWLEDGEMENTS

Raymond McCartney; Gavin and Tina McClurg; Mary and Maura McConnell; Johnnie and Teresa McKeagney; Joanna McVey; John and Marion Maxwell; Arthur and Eleanor Mitchell; Kathleen and Michael Murphy; Kevin Myers; Margaret O'Donnell; Joy Parke; William K. Parke; the staff of the Peace and Reconciliation Group; Charlie Pierce; Richard Pierce; Helen Quinn; Sean Quinn, the staff of Quinn's Cement Works and Frank Kavanagh; the late Brian Reihill, Mary Reihill and Jane, Clare and Ramona Reihill; Val and Mary Rogers; George Sheridan; Billie and Stella Talbot; Nigel Tilson; Liz Ann and Elizabeth Treacy; Mrs White; Chief Inspector W. C. S. White; all of the Williams family; Wilma Williamson; Lenni Brown Reid, who helped with the preparation of the manuscript; Joan Trimble for her advice on the manuscript; and of course my family, who came with me. Finally I am particularly grateful to those people who took personal risks to help me, and it is in the nature of things that I cannot mention them by name. All mistakes of course are my own.

Carlo Gébler

Rossfad
Co. Fermanagh
21 March 1991

The thirty-two counties, four provinces and main cities of
Ireland together with the North-South border

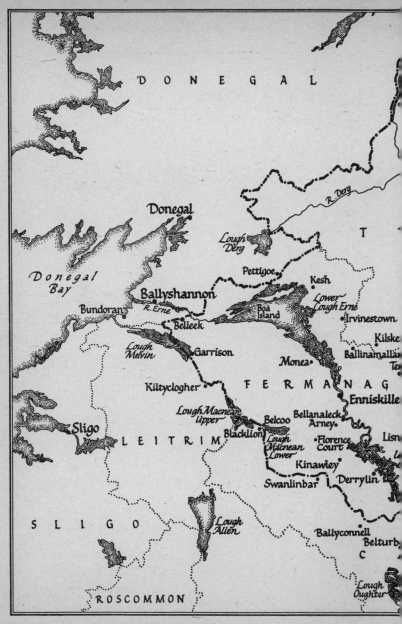

Co. Fermanagh and nearby counties

Derry

Border between the Republic of Ireland and Northern Ireland

0   10   20 miles
0   10   20   30 km

L O N D O N D E R R Y

N

O N E

Lough
Neagh

Augher

Clogher
ivemiletown

D O W N

Armagh

keborough

A R M A G H

Rosslea

Keady

town
er

M O N A G H A N

Clones

Newry

Castleblayney

A N

L O U T H

Dundalk

Glossary

Apprentice Boys of Derry: Protestant organization

Ard-Fheis: national convention of any Irish organization.

B-Specials: armed auxiliary police force and part of the Ulster Special Constabulary. Disbanded 1970. Also known as B-Men

barracks: police station

Dáil Éireann: lower house of the parliament of the Republic of Ireland in Dublin (the Senate is the upper house)

DUP: Democratic Unionist Party

Fenian: Republican/Nationalist/Catholic. Can be pejorative

Garda Síochána: Irish police force

Green: Republican/Nationalist/Catholic

IRA: Irish Republican Army. Founded earlier in the century to fight for a 32-county independent Irish state. In 1970 it split into Official and Provisional IRA, with the Officials favouring political rather than military action and generally holding left-wing views. Since May 1972 the Officials have observed a ceasefire. Sinn Féin (q.v.) is the IRA's political wing

Orange: Loyalist/Unionist/Protestant

Orange Order: Protestant organization

OUP: Official Unionist Party

Preceptory: unit within the Royal Black Institution

Provos/Provies: Provisional IRA (*see* IRA)

punts: Irish pounds

RBI: Royal Black Institution; effectively the senior branch of the Orange Order

RIC: Royal Irish Constabulary, disbanded in 1922, replaced by the Garda Síochána in the Free State and by the RUC in Northern Ireland

RUC: Royal Ulster Constabulary

SDLP: Social Democratic and Labour Party

Sinn Féin: translates from the Irish as 'Ourselves Alone'. Political party aspiring to full Irish independence, as well as acting as the political wing of the IRA (q.v.). Like the IRA, Sinn Féin split into Official and Provisional groups; the Officials have always had a more left-wing orientation

Stickies: Official IRA (*see* IRA). The term derives from the practice of sticking lilies on coat lapels at Easter 1916 celebrations

Taig: pejorative term for a Roman Catholic

TD: member of the Dáil

UDA: Ulster Defence Association (legal Protestant paramilitary organization)

UDR: Ulster Defence Regiment. A regular regiment of the British Army, recruited and permanently based in Northern Ireland

UFF: Ulster Freedom Fighters (illegal Protestant paramilitary organization)

UVF: Ulster Volunteer Force (illegal Protestant paramilitary organization)

VCP: vehicle checkpoint

The whole map of Europe has been changed. The mode and thought of men, the whole outlook on affairs, the grouping of parties, all have encountered violent and tremendous changes in the deluge of the world, but as the deluge subsides and the waters fall, we see the dreary steeples of Fermanagh and Tyrone emerging once again. The integrity of their quarrel is one of the few institutions that has been left unaltered in the cataclysm which has swept the world.

Winston Churchill, *The Aftermath*, 1929

Introduction

I

When I started this book, I imagined I was going to write a biography of the town of Enniskillen and its hinterland, Co. Fermanagh. I decided that as every biographer talks to relatives if he can, I would be no exception. This would allow me to stray beyond the territorial limits of the subject. Also, like many biographies, mine would have a chronological spine, although, since the subject was not dead, I would have to be selective. I chose the year running from July 1989 to July 1990. So far so good. Yet when I came out at the other end, I found what I had was not at all what I imagined I would have when I began, and to have called it then a biography of Enniskillen would have been to impose a description which no longer fitted. So I dropped the idea, subtitling it 'Inside an Ulster Community' instead.

II

A Northern Ireland, or Ulster, community (I use the terms interchangeably) is a controversial subject (like the best biographical subjects). That being so, it is useful for the reader to have some knowledge of the writer and of the mental baggage he carries with him before they embark together on their journey, just as in, say, a conversation about the existence of God it is helpful for the interlocutors to be unambiguous about whether or not they believe. Ireland, in many ways, is like a theological issue, and positions are a matter of faith.

What follows is necessarily autobiographical, but I will make it as short as possible.

*

I was born in Dublin. I was baptized a Catholic to placate family, but there was no religious practice in the home; in fact, if anything there was a positive antagonism to organized religion, although not to the spirit of religion. However, in one of the places where I spent part of my childhood, Co. Clare, I found myself among believers, with the consequence that I became adept at going through the motions of religious observance (much like a prisoner learns to show contrition and whatever else the regime requires). This pleased my grandparents, whose original desire it had been that my brother and I be baptized.

As I grew up, the impression of Northern Ireland which I absorbed was that it was the 'Black North', full of hard-nosed Presbyterians who were good at business but not much else. There was little discussion, pre-1969, that is, of the fate of Catholics in the Unionist state (or statelet, as it was sarcastically called). Partition, however, was frequently raked over. The subject produced much chagrin and a lot of breast-beating. The national propensity to cock things up, so our discussions went, combined with Anglo-Saxon cunning, had denied Ireland her wholeness by keeping six of Ulster's nine counties under the Crown. On the other hand, not only was there a grudging recognition that sometimes matters were better organized in heathen England and, by association, Ulster (the National Health Service for instance), a recognition which tended to undermine confidence, but there was also a sense that while in theory a 32-county state was to be desired, in practice it raised certain problems. Such as, did we really seriously believe we could carry the Protestants kicking and screaming into a United Ireland? And what were we meant to do with them once we had? Therefore, in the milieu in which I found myself – rural, prosperous and Fianna

Fáil(ish) our attitude to the North emphasized the *pragmatic* (a word always stressed to ward off accusations of cowardliness from hardliners). Yes, a United Ireland in principle, we said, but not immediately. For God's sake, let's first get right the bit we've got, before we take on any more.

Then came 1969. I was sixteen that year. I wondered what was going on up there, as the rioting, bombings and shootings became nightly occurrences. Bloody Sunday tipped the balance, emotionally at any rate, towards the Nationalists and against the state; but, in the months and years which followed, that balance started to tip away from them (although not towards the Unionists – to tip towards them was inconceivable). It was kangaroo justice – especially the treatment of girls who had 'erred' by becoming involved with British soldiers – and the indiscriminate bombings which weighted the other side of the scales for me. It was partly a matter of squeamishness, but there was also a principle involved here. I had grown up with the remark (was it Dan Breen in *My Fight for Irish Freedom?*) 'You can't make an omelette without breaking eggs', something that had been said of the IRA campaign in the twenties; but since that time the idea that the ends justified the means no longer had the same cachet. So why in Northern Ireland was there a return to this discredited concept?

I started to visit Northern Ireland in the mid seventies and continued to do so through the eighties. During my visits, if I learned anything, it was about the complexity of the situation. While one is always prepared to admit to this in theory, it is none the less bewildering when confronted with it head-on, as was the case for me during a dance in a small village in Co. Leitrim, two miles from the border, during the hunger strike. While the Provisional IRA hijacked an oil-delivery lorry and set fire to it outside, I was questioned inside by two Stickies, men whose patriotism I never doubted, until, during the Irish national anthem, they lowered their trousers and showed their buttocks to the band.

In 1989 I moved to the North with the intention of finding out what the place was really like, choosing the countryside rather than Belfast, because it seemed to me it was ground which had been less exhaustively covered. The experience of arriving in Fermanagh was like being parachuted into a strange country. At first I was lost and I didn't speak the language, but gradually with time I gained knowledge and some sort of fluency. In a land of many signs I learned to understand and read some of them at least, a process that I have attempted to describe.

Finally, a caveat. This is a book with as little history as it is possible to have in any book about Ireland.

Prologue

I was in Enniskillen, having a look around. I had never been there before, and what I knew about the place could easily have fitted on the back of a postcard. This was: Enniskillen was a place where a bomb planted by the IRA had killed eleven people at the 1987 Remembrance Sunday parade; it was the home town of a remarkable man called Gordon Wilson who had lost a daughter in the explosion, but who had appeared on television that Sunday evening and stated he had prayed for the murderers of his daughter, and that, far from seeking retribution, he forgave them (which inspired the phrase 'the Spirit of Enniskillen'); it was a town with a long tradition of service in the British Army (which perhaps was why the bomb had been planted there in the first place) and enjoyed the unique distinction of being the only town in the British Isles to have provided not one but two regiments; and, finally, it was a town in a constituency – Fermanagh-South Tyrone – where support for Sinn Féin was so strong that hunger striker Bobby Sands had been elected MP in April 1981, and, after he died, his agent Owen Carron had captured the seat. I think this spread of information is what most people, those who know of the existence of Enniskillen anyway, carry around in their heads.

The information I had was also guessed at by my guide – a Catholic – but then natives always know the exact perimeters of the outsider's knowledge. She navigated me to the place which she knew I would instantly recognize from television and said, 'This was where the bomb was.'

Outside the car window the war memorial flashed by. I

recognized the figure on the pedestal with its bowed head from the news broadcasts following the bombing in 1987. Simultaneously I recalled the video of the minutes immediately after the bomb, shot by an amateur, which was also widely shown at the time. It was a hectic, frantic piece of footage and a rare example of unsanitized television. This was not because of what it showed – indeed the bodies of the dead were only fleetingly glimpsed in it – but because what the cameraman did with his video recorder during the shooting, the way he waved it around and was completely unable to focus, conveyed better than any words what the profound shock induced by violence is actually like. The video was a far more severe comment on the bombing than that given by any pundit. Furthermore, watching the piece, I recognized that had I been in the position of the amateur who shot it, I would have reacted similarly and produced the same sort of result. And while I was thinking about all of this, I was also looking out of the car window and finding it hard to believe this was the same place I had seen on television.

We drove up the main street, crowded with shoppers, and over a new bridge.

'You know they wanted to name this after Bobby Sands,' said my guide.

I remembered his funeral, May 1981; an estimated 20,000 lined the route from Twinbrook, West Belfast, to Milltown Cemetery. The turn-out so frightened the British government, I had heard it said, that they came up with the Anglo-Irish Agreement.

We passed into the countryside. The sun sparkled behind the hedgerows; lines of beech and oak marched across the top of hills; the grass in the fields was dark green. Every few yards there were glimpses of lakes, streams and rivers, rimmed by reeds and groves of alder trees.

Yet only a few miles south of this idyllic landscape, if I was to believe the Sunday colour supplements, Protestant farmers in their houses along the border were under siege from the IRA. Because of death threats they rode to work like latterday cowboys, loaded shotguns beside them in their tractor cabs. Was that really happening here?

'This is Ballinamallard,' said my guide, as we came into a village. 'It's 100 per cent Loyal. They don't like Catholics to come and live here.'

So here it was, the legendary place with the fearsome reputation for Protestant exclusivity and the stage-Irish name, which I had often heard my friends around the Province chortling over. I stared out of the window, so that I could report back to them on what I had seen, but this most Irish-sounding of strongholds gave not a hint of where its loyalties lay. There was not even a Union flag fluttering from a lamp-post or a gable-end daubed 'No Surrender'. It was just like any other Irish village: a place of small, grey, crouched houses.

RESEARCH

I started looking for something to read about the county but could turn up almost nothing.

Television was not much better. The only time Fermanagh made an appearance was as a backdrop to a border killing.

(1) *Pan* over green fields
(2) *Close-up* of abandoned car with shattered windscreen
(3) *Long shot* of body bag being hauled into a helicopter

Alternatively, Fermanagh was a mention in a tourist brochure, illustrated by a picture of water lit up by sunshine.

REMEMBRANCE SUNDAY

Remembrance Sunday, 1988, was the first anniversary of the Enniskillen bombing. I arrived on the Saturday night beforehand. Armoured cars and Land Rovers were at VCPs on all the roads into town. I parked the car and in seconds was surrounded by heavily armed policemen. I showed my driving licence again (fourth time that day) and walked up to the main street. Soldiers in every doorway, soldiers on every rooftop, soldiers coming out of drains. In front of each shop its owner stood, waiting for an army search party to check his premises. Sniffer dogs barked, torches flashed in shop windows, squaddies and RUC men conversed in a low susurrus. There was not a single civilian in sight, but when I went into a pub, it was full of them.

After a drink I went on to Irvinestown, where I was staying.

*

The next morning the wet road shone in the sun as I drove back to Enniskillen. The tarmac was blue-black, like the sheen on a crow.

In town I parked near the cattle market and got out to walk. Every four or five yards stood a knot of men in the dark green RUC uniform, poppies tucked in the bands of their peaked hats.

One side of the war memorial was cordoned off for the press with crush barriers. There were hours to go, but the photographers from Fleet Street were already there, sitting on stepladders, their cameras with their proboscis-like lenses before them.

Suddenly two soldiers with rifles appeared. The photographers immediately started snapping. The soldiers were a strong image with the figure on the top of the war memorial in the background. However, I though the real story was the policemen in the empty streets amid those comforting tokens of Britishness, the red pillar-boxes and the hoardings advertising the Bradford & Bingley Building Society.

*

At half past ten, four UDR men and a sergeant marched from the direction of the High Street and took up positions around the memorial.

A hush fell. Rooks on the telegraph wires cawed for a moment or two, but then they too fell silent. Soldiers skirting a house knocked against something, perhaps a can, and called out, 'Sorry,' they were so embarrassed. The journalist on the wall beside me wrote in his notebook 'spooky'.

We waited and waited and finally, coming from the direction of Gaol Square, music. It was the Ballyreagh Silver Band. When they reached the memorial, they stopped playing, marked time on the spot to the tapping of a single drum, wheeled 180 degrees around the base of the podium, then came to a halt.

More units appeared, and each repeated this wheeling to the rhythm of a single drum. In my notebook I wrote, 'Footsteps like taps of rain on glass.' Then I wrote '*auto-da-fé*' as an *aide-mémoire* to the strange, sanctified, quasi-religious atmosphere.

In the British Legion ranks there were men with banners, which they now raised and lowered. Bells were tolling in the distance. A figure in a suit with medals pinned to his chest kept checking his watch.

'Remove head-dress,' he shouted. A bugler started to play 'The Last Post'. I would not have thought it possible that the crowds could be stiller than they had been, but they were. Only the camera shutters and the motorized film drives moved.

'At the going down of the sun and in the morning we will remember them,' intoned a figure when the music finished.

'When you go home, tell them of us and say, "For your tomorrow, we gave our today,"' said another.

The wreath-laying followed: the British Legion in groups of three on one side, civilians on the other. It all went like clockwork until a Girl Guide lost her shoe, and jumped down from the perimeter wall.

The music stopped when the wreath-laying was over. The players cleared the spittle from their instruments and marched away. The press headed up the street towards St Macartin's Cathedral, where the official service would shortly be held.

Many locals surged round the memorial to read the inscriptions on the wreaths and to take photographs.

I followed the press up the High Street. At the top the entrance to the Church of Ireland cathedral was jammed, and I noticed a number of journalists crossing the road and going into the Methodist church opposite. This was Gordon Wilson's church, but I didn't know that then, as I hurried over and entered.

I collected a hymn book inside the door and found a seat in the gallery upstairs beside a lady from the Salvation Army. The minister was a balding man with a red pate. He wore an extraordinary voluminous black outfit and a white tie at the neck.

After the hymns the minister, the Revd Tom Magowan, delivered his address. It was his fervent hope, he said, that the media would withdraw from Enniskillen and allow those who had suffered from the outrage to come to terms with their grief in peace and without intrusion. I tried to gauge whether his view was received favourably by the congregation, but I could not tell. Everyone simply sat and listened politely, as if constrained by their collective sense that though this was a religious ceremony, it was also, like the whole day, an artificially staged event for those of us who had come to gawp.

After the service I walked back down through the town. The 'No Parking' cones and the temporary barriers were being packed away into lorries. Soldiers scrambled into the belly of a helicopter near the river. The gawpers were leaving town.

I decided I would return to write about Enniskillen, but that I would observe two conditions: the bombing would be only a part, rather than the centre, of any work; and I would not seek out the survivors.

Diary

The day after this Remembrance Sunday a man who has lost his family in the bombing and been badly injured himself is in a pub. He is wearing a poppy. Four men threaten trouble if he does not go. The 'English poppy', as they refer to it, is not welcome. Only after he has left is it discovered what has happened.

I am told the story by the owner of the bar. 'I could have kicked myself,' she says. 'I should have spotted it coming and stopped it before it even started.' She and the manager, both Catholics, are outraged that these 'Sinn Féiners' threatened a customer because he wore a poppy. 'Next year we'll have one ourselves and that'll be the end of that,' she says.

*

At a quiet get-together of transvestites in Belfast, a handbag is stolen.

'I'm calling the police,' says the woman whose property it was.

'No, you don't, you police-loving bitch. We're not having the forces of the Crown in here,' shouts a lady from the 'other side of the house'.

Within seconds the two camps are brawling. A true story.

Part One

Summer

I

The Way to Ireland

In the still hours in the middle of the night in London we heard them – the Lisburn lads from the corner house at the end of the road. They were shouting, breaking bottles and pissing in the gutters.

The next morning we woke to the fruits of their nocturnal exuberance. On the hoarding fronting the flats at the top of the street they had written in huge letters with a spray can

Fuck the Pope and the IRA
All the way with the UDA

and on the wall of a neighbour's house

KILL the IRA. They are Murdering Scum and Bastards

That same morning we loaded the luggage into the car and left for Northern Ireland.

THE NEXT DAY

In the Scottish port of Stranraer the sun was sparkling on the waters of the Irish Sea, but the car deck of the ferry was gloomy. It smelled of rotten fish and petrol fumes, and it echoed with the shouts and jeers of drunken young men.

'You can go into the motorists' lounge,' whispered a security guard confidentially. Handcuffs dangled from his belt. 'You'll be quite safe from "them" in there.'

The 'them' were Orangemen from Scotland, who were travelling to Northern Ireland for the marching the next day, which was the Twelfth. Now I understood what had been up with our boys from Lisburn two nights before. They had been getting in the mood.

*

A customs declaration of some of the literary works I was about to take over the water with me.

Who Killed Palomino Molero? is a short novel by Mario Vargas Llosa which I had not been able to forget. It tells the story of a murder investigation in a Peruvian provincial town in the 1950s. Great emphasis is made in the novel on the conspiracy theories, mostly of a leftish nature, which the local people come up with to explain what has happened. In the end it turns out the murder is a crime of passion and not a political act. Yet even after the truth emerges the local people can't bring themselves to accept this, insisting, 'It had to do with contraband, that it was a spy story. That Ecuador was involved.'* They do this with the same puzzling persistence that some people today continue to declare the earth is flat.

Vargas Llosa is well known for being a man of the right; in 1989 he stood in the Peruvian presidential election as their candidate. Yet this is not an explicitly right-wing or polemical book tilting at leftists alone, and it contains no caricature Maoists. Rather it is a fable, albeit written realistically, with a message which anyone, regardless of his position on the political spectrum, can accept. All people, he says, are capable of succumbing to poisonous fantasies which no amount of reality – no matter how strong the dose – can shift them from, no

* *Who Killed Palomino Molero?* p. 150.

more than photographs of the earth taken from the moon can shake the flat-earthers from their beliefs.

*

A Place Apart by Dervla Murphy, a travel book, is the best modern study of Ulster.

In search of the soul of the Province, Dervla Murphy spent a good deal of time with the extremists on both sides. It is undeniable that they were, and still are, the thread which colours the cloth. However, since she covered the ground so thoroughly, and since the 'hard men' are not much changed since she wrote about them, I made the decision to do something different. This was partially to avoid repetition, but more because I wouldn't have been able to do it as well as she did. I would go for the cloth, I decided, the background against which the bright threads of the paramilitaries stand out, but without which they would not exist.

*

Following the security guard's advice, we went to the motorists' lounge. It was large, clean and empty, except for half a dozen other middle-class refugees. We found a place in the corner and spread ourselves along the seats.

Exclusivity is always provocative, and what happened next was inevitable. The door from the deck was flung open and in surged ninety or a hundred urban followers of Bacchus. They were naked from the waist up, had hard, white, tattooed bodies, and were laden with drink. They took every available seat. Some lay on the floor. The Orangemen who came to our corner carried silver sacks ripped from wine boxes. They drank from these as if they were gourds, holding them at arm's length and squirting jets into their open mouths.

On the other side of the room someone lit a cigarette. The smoker was a youth in a pair of blue, shimmery tracksuit trousers.

'Excuse me! This is a no-smoking area,' called the middle-aged man sitting behind me in an educated Edinburgh accent, while pointing at the prominent notice.

The youth ignored him. The man rose to his feet. The motorists' lounge fell absolutely silent. The man walked round and bent over the smoker.

'In case you can't read English, Jock, that sign means no smoking.'

There was a very, very long pause before the smoker nonchalantly dropped his fag into an empty can, where it spluttered and went out.

Another pause and then somebody broke the unbearable atmosphere by pulling the ring on a can of Special Brew. A salvo of further hisses followed, mixed with the phuts of whisky-bottle screw caps being opened. A ghetto blaster was turned on, and from the speakers drifted 'The Sash':

> Here am I, a loy-al-O-range man, just come a-cross the sea,
> For sing-ing and for danc-ing I hope that I'll please thee,
> I can sing and dance with an-y man as I did in days of yore,
> And it's on the Twelfth I love to wear the sash my fa-ther
>   wore.

Some Orangemen took out their instruments and began to play along with the tape.

'Like the zoo, isn't it?' I heard. It was the wife of the anti-smoking crusader.

'I'm sorry?'

'I said, like the zoo,' she shouted over the hubbub and pointed at my two-year-old son.

When I saw his expression, as he stared out into the room, I understood what she meant. It was the zoo to him.

It was not, however, a spectacle to my daughter, India. She was older and wiser at eight than he was at two, and the worry showed on her pale face. She had her Snoopy letter-pad open on the table in front of her and had written 'Dear Holly' at the top, but then nervousness had paralysed her, and she had not been able to write another word.

'How's it going?' asked the Orangeman on the seat beside her.

Not surprisingly she moved away from him. He was in his early twenties and bore the marks of a recent fight: two black eyes, a swollen lip and a broken nose. He followed her along the seat.

'Take a letter,' he said and smiled. He glanced down at the pad. '"Dear Holly."' India looked uncertain, then moved her pen to the next line, ready to write. '"I am on a boat,"' he dictated. '"I am surrounded by a lot of Orangemen. They are making too much noise and drinking too much . . ."'

A long letter followed, describing where we were and the antics of the Orangemen as they sang, wrestled, joked, shouted and even slept, which she copied slowly in her round, large handwriting. By the time she came to write 'Yours, with lots of love' at the bottom of the page, she had grown calm.

'Where are you going to march?' I asked him when the dictation was finished.

'Lurgan first, then Keady; it's 90 per cent Catholic there, I hear, but we're not going to make trouble. Only out for a bit of fun, aren't we? If the Catholics'll let us.'

There was a twinkle in his eye, but he was drinking Iron-Brew, unlike the rest of the cabin, who were all on lager, vodka, whisky and wine, and he didn't smell of alcohol.

'Where are you from?' he asked.

'Dublin.'

'Picked the wrong day for travelling, didn't you?'

'Did I? Everyone looks friendly to me.'

'What's Dublin like?' he asked.

'Well . . .' I began but got no further, because the next moment a hundred pairs of lungs started to chant, 'Fuck you, Mo, fuck you, Mo, fuck you, Mo . . .' Mo was Maurice Johnston, the first Catholic in Scottish football history to sign to Rangers, a club with a distinctly Loyalist and Protestant identity. Mo's timing was immaculate; he had done it just the day before.

'What do you think about the Anglo-Irish Agreement?' he asked.

I cannot remember what I said. I do remember he interrupted.

'How would you feel, if you were British, and these Irish people began trying to make you stop being British and to start being Irish? You wouldn't like it, would you?'

He's nice, then a nut, but the same person all the way through, I thought as I started to reply, and then he interrupted again.

'Once we start talking to you Catholic people, we get lulled into this false sense of security. But all the time we're talking to you, you're really stealing up behind us, and then, wallop, you have us.'

I know when it's time to leave. We fled to the 'Paddle Steamer', the children's playroom in the bowels of the ship. It was filled with bright plastic toys and frightened Catholics trying to act cool. Then someone was sick. The smell was unbearable. We decided to risk the decks.

Although they were thronged, we felt less anxious outside than we had felt sitting in the motorists' lounge. We sauntered about. Everyone was wearing William of Orange T-shirts and UVF caddy hats, and everyone seemed to be tattooed with the Loyalist acronyms UDA, UVF, UFF. Towards the bow three Swedish hitch-hikers, looking like extras from a *Carry On* film, lay in the sun.

'Where'd-ya-get-the-gear?' an Orangeman asked one.

She was puzzled. 'I am sorry. Please to speak again.'

'Where'd-you-get-the-gear?'

'Ah, my clo-thes, you mean. This, I am wearing, is the Adidas of Sweden.'

'Wanna-come-an-have-a-bevy?' He linked his arm through hers, and she let him lead her off.

I was relieved that at least sex had triumphed over narrow

sectarian allegiance on the *Princess of Galloway*. On the other hand, as I reflected a few minutes later, being a Swede, she was probably a Calvinist like him.

LANDFALL

We disembarked at Larne. Brilliant clear skies; kerbstones newly painted the colours of the Union flag, red, white and blue, ready for the following day; bunting with the same colour scheme stretching between the houses; and, swaying above one street, a banner, a beautiful piece of folk art, showing King Billy on his charger, imperiously pointing the way forward. Girls in short skirts. Young men in coloured bermudas. In a burned-out petrol station a family of tinkers were camped between rusting pumps, their washing stretched across the forecourt to dry in the sun. Further on prosperity and neatness again. Clipped grass verges. Tidy front gardens with flowers growing in neat rows. Garages with the doors open and views of the contents: hoses neatly coiled, shining barbecue griddles, rolls of wire netting.

Out of town, rolling hills crowned with neat white farm-houses. Farmyards with sheds of green and red corrugated iron. John Deere tractors parked in neat lines in neat lanes. Outside another village a placard hung from a lamp-post, reading 'Ulster Says NO', while two Union Jacks fluttered over the Presbyterian church. Then more painted kerbstones; more bunting; and another banner, this one showing Queen Elizabeth surrounded by a circle of Sweet William and orange gladioli; also more shields on lamp-posts, these ones emblazoned 'UVF 1912–89' and 'Ulster' above a picture of the 'Red Hand', a hand (bloodstained by tradition) palm up and fingers outstretched (the classic 'no' or 'stop' position, as many commentators have observed), and a symbol of the Province which often features in Loyalist or Unionist material; then finally, on the village outskirts, lest there should be any misunderstanding as to whom the territory belonged, the simple message,

Taigs Beware

with a gallows underneath and a stick man hanging by his neck.

In between these showcases the housing estates of the 'other side' (especially as we came into Belfast): green, white and gold kerbstones (echoing the Irish tricolour) and freshly painted in readiness for their own marching season; gable-end paintings of Gaelic chieftains standing shoulder to shoulder with balaclava-clad 'freedom fighters' wielding Armalites (an obvious attempt to link the current situation to the mythical past); doves trapped in barbed wire; the Nationalists' riposte to the Protestants' 'No Surrender', 'Our Time Shall Come'; and this chilling line – as chilling as 'Taigs Beware' although wittier – which I saw on the wall in West Belfast:

Semtex kills more germs than Vortex

In my notebook I wrote, 'All very interesting, colourful and alarming – two cultures shouting through their emblems vociferously at one another and yet not having the slightest interest in communicating.' We got through Belfast and pointed ourselves towards our destination: Enniskillen.

Diary

His father is from Scotland and his mother from Co. Fermanagh. 'I'm a bit of an international,' he says.

He is born in Cumberland, but when he is seven, his father dies, and his mother comes home with her two sons. The year is 1927.

They rent a house near the Five Points and then move to the house where I am talking to him. At this time it is a thatched cottage in bad repair. They can get things fixed up only whenever they have a few pounds to spare. The house was not slated until after the Second World War.

We are in a small room at the back of the house. A girl of about eight comes in with a tray of tea and cakes.

'Your granddaughter,' I say.

'No, my daughter,' he replies.

I am puzzled. I know he is sixty-nine. He tells me then that he did not marry until late in life. 'Why didn't you marry earlier?' I ask.

'I liked the free life. And I needed to get the money that I knew I was going to need if I was going to keep going when I was married.'

Then he tells me he still does not know how much younger his wife is than he is. Sixteen or seventeen years, he thinks, but that is only a guess, he admits.

In my notebook I write, 'Everything topsy-turvy.'

2

History

1066 and All That was a wonderful title and wonderfully true. 1066 was the only date that was undoubtedly known to everyone who had passed through the English school system. It was also *the* date. Pre-1066, the Romans notwithstanding, was the time of the Dark Ages, before history. Post-1066, with the coming of the Normans and the civilization they introduced, was the start of history. 1066 was the dividing line.

Had W.C. Seller and R.J. Yeatman turned to Ireland and her past, they would not have found the subject so tractable. What date could they have chosen which would have been *the* date, a beginning for Irish history upon which every Irish reader could agree?

1170 Invasion of Ireland by the Normans
1610 Plantation of Ulster
1641 Ulster Rebellion. Massacre of Protestants
1649 Cromwell retaliates and massacres Drogheda and Wexford
1690 Battle of the Boyne. William defeats James II. Penal Laws follow
1798 Uprising of United Irishmen
1801 Union of Great Britain and Ireland to produce the United Kingdom
1914 Curragh Mutiny. British Army refuses to move against Ulster Volunteer Force and impose Home Rule
1916 Easter Uprising

1921 Anglo-Irish War ends with formation of Irish Free State and Northern Ireland

There are just too many choices.

Diary

A story from the 1960s pre-dating the current round of the Troubles.

Miss Noreen Cooper, daughter of one of the Coopers of Cooper & Cooper, a long-established firm of Enniskillen solicitors, drives a car, registration number IL 1690 (Battle of the Boyne and numinous date in Protestant annals).

Before long Senator O'Hare, a Nationalist and editor of a local newspaper, the Fermanagh Herald, is driving a car, registration number IL 1798 (United Irishmen uprising and numinous date in Catholic annals).

It is a witty riposte, I assume, until I discover IL 1798 was assigned O'Hare by some Protestant wag in the Vehicle Registration Office. This part of the story, on all the occasions it is told to me (which are several), is never mentioned.

3

First Impressions

SIR ANTHONY'S ADMIRER

On our first evening in Enniskillen we went out. In the restaurant a customer, mistaking me for my cousin Stan Gebler Davies, asked me if it wasn't provocative and reckless to have stood in the 1987 Irish elections as the prospective Conservative and Unionist candidate for the constituency of Cork South-west. As it was, he had not stood but simply published a jokey election manifesto in the *Spectator*, which I pointed out.* I felt mildly irritated that, within hours of arriving, I was already being coded.

The conversation with the stranger continued. Inevitably she asked, 'Are you enjoying your holidays?'

'Actually, we've come here to live for a while.'

'I see.'

Her next question was one I was to hear many times in the future, as strangers probed to know which foot I kicked with, that is, my religion.

'What school for the kiddies?' she inquired.

Unfortunately my answer denied her the information she was seeking. My daughter India was going to the Integrated, a brand-new school due to open its doors in a month, where children of all faiths would be educated.

'It's a good idea,' she said, sounding tired suddenly, 'but what'll it achieve? What's the point of a school for the enlightened?'

'And your own children?'

* *Spectator*, 31 January 1987.

'Grown up now, thank goodness.'

She sighed and told her story. Her daughter had been doing badly at a Catholic secondary school. So she took drastic action and sent her to Portora Royal (then a noted local public school – the 'Eton of Ireland' it was sometimes called – today a voluntary grammar school).

'No one ever said anything to me directly, but there was outrage on our side of the house. It was a betrayal sending her to an "English public school".'

'Would you do it again?'

'No way.'

Later she told me she was reading the life of Sir Anthony Eden.

'He was a lovely man,' she said, 'a real English gentleman . . .'

THE TOWN

Enniskillen, the county town of Fermanagh, occupies an island shaped like a three-cornered hat, caught in the web of waterways that connect Lower and Upper Lough Erne. Inniskillen, the name of the island, is also the name of two celebrated Irish regiments, the 27th (Inniskilling) Fusiliers and the 6th (Inniskilling) Dragoons, though the town has now changed the I for an E. Since the war most of the old houses on the island have been demolished and the inhabitants moved across the Erne to estates on the mainland.

An exception, however, was John. Until he was sixteen, his family had lived over his uncle's barber shop on Darling Street, so he could claim to be a real Inniskillener. He had thick black hair and dark blue eyes.

We met at the top of the tallest hill. On one side of the road stood St Michael's, the Catholic parish church, a Gothic-revival building with a smooth, grey, stone front. Bang opposite was St Macartin's, the Protestant cathedral. It was begun by Captain (later Sir William) Cole, an English soldier who was appointed constable in 1607 by James I. One of the conditions of his appointment was that he build on and develop the island. He did, but, like all his buildings, the church was much altered, and what stands today is solid and mainly Victorian.*

We sauntered down the hill and along the main street. It was lined with more solid Victorian three-storey dwellings, mostly painted a variety of pastel colours. It was a long way from Churchill's Fermanagh of 'dreary steeples'. Then John said, 'You'll have noticed there aren't any rubbish bins.' I had not. He explained: in 1987, a reserve constable called Ivan Crawford had been killed by a remote-controlled bomb left in a litter bin. The authorities took them all away after that.†

At the far end of the main street lay the East Bridge, and on the mainland side stood the war memorial. There was one wreath of red poppies. This was the site where on Remembrance Sunday, 1987, a bomb killed eleven and injured sixty-three people who were waiting for the annual ceremony to begin.

'I'm going to be ghoulish,' I said. I climbed on to a wall and looked down into the ruins of the St Michael's Reading Rooms where the bomb had been left. John hung back. I saw rubble, broken floorboards, twisted conduit. Chaos.

'Come and look at this,' John called.

Turning our backs on the memorial, we looked over the side of the bridge. On the river bank below there was an oval-shaped plot of land surrounded by a stone wall and planted with trees. Until the level of the lake was lowered several feet in the last century, he explained, this had been the island of Enniskillen from where the town had got its name, and by tradition it had been inhabited by native Irish a thousand

---

* Alistair Rowan, *North West Ulster*, pp. 276–7.
† At this moment of writing they are making a come-back.

years before Sir William Cole and the Planters came. This was pre-Plantation Enniskillen, and it lay, literally, just under the memorial, symbol of military service to the Crown. Catholic and Protestant, Gaelic and Planter – the two traditions were twenty feet apart.

GOSSIP

For lunch we went to a bar, where John introduced me to Mr Holland. For my benefit, Mr Holland immediately began to appraise all the public houses and restaurants in the county.

'I suppose you heard about –?' he said.

I remembered passing the place on a previous visit and nodded.

'The IRA blew it up. They said the owner was serving members of the security services. I don't know whether it's true or not,' he whispered.

He was a small round fellow, with leathery skin and a pink tongue. He reminded me of a lizard.

'It was just a wee Fermanagh place before it was blown up, but now it's pretty impressive, isn't it?'

I did remember thinking on my last visit that it was vast, opulent-looking and somewhat unexpected in context.

'And of course you heard about –?' he continued, mentioning another place I cannot mention. I had, at least about its being bombed.

'I find that very interesting too.' He rolled his tongue around his lips. 'The IRA said they were serving members of the security services as well. And I bet they'll have a lovely new place next year, and all paid for by the Northern Ireland Office from my taxes and your taxes, thank you very much.'

He squeezed my arm and scuttled off.

'What exactly was that about?'

'He wants you to know,' said John, 'that (A) the IRA are a

mafia; (B) the proprietors who pay to have their premises bombed are totally irresponsible; and (C) the whole bloody thing's a waste of money which could be better spent on, let's say, building houses.' He paused and continued, 'It's a funny thing, anywhere else, when compensation's coming from an insurance company or the government, most people's attitude would be, "Get every penny that can be got." But when it comes to what Mr Holland is talking about, all that goes out the window. Some don't like the way the Northern Ireland Office is ripped off in this way.'

PRICES

The next moment John nudged me, and through the door sailed two ladies with woollen tea-cosy hats on their heads.

'Menu, please,' demanded one.

The manager obliged.

'I haven't got my glasses,' she said. 'How much is this?' She pointed.

'Two fifty,' he said.

'No, I don't think we'll stay,' said the other, and they turned to leave.

At that moment the waitress, with our meals, came from the direction of the kitchen.

'I lost 'em,' the manager called out ruefully to her.

*

After lunch we crossed over Johnston Bridge and turned into Corban Avenue towards Kilmacormick One Estate. There was a block on our right, its shops boarded up and its flats abandoned. Posters of Danny Morrison, the Sinn Féin candidate in the 1989 European Parliament election, stared down at us. There was a feeble picture of the Irish tricolour on a wall and another of a phoenix with a message about Ireland's freedom. The Irish flag hung limply from a lamp-post.

'Would Ken Maginnis canvas here at election time?'*

'I shouldn't think so. It wouldn't be worth his while, and besides, it would be seen as provocative.'

On the porch of a house there was a line of gnomes, the paint flaking from them. In a garden a stack of turf was sheeted with polythene bags. In a dog run the grass was scraped back to bare earth and scattered with black turds and bits of broken bone. Radios and television sets boomed in every house. A broken window was fixed with a blanket and pieces of cardboard. Men stood around in silent knots or walked furiously, rolled-up newspapers in their pockets, as they killed the hours to opening time or dinner. This was the moment when I understood why our lunch had cost three pounds for both of us.

Diary

Returning from the cinema, the Ritz, where we have just seen Batman, *we come on a temporary VCP. One of the policemen on duty is canvassing opinions on the film from everyone in front of us, and we have to wait five or ten minutes before he waves us forward.*

'Well, what do yous think of Batman?' *he asks, disdaining the offer of a driving licence and leaning on our open window. 'The ones in front say it's no good. What do you say?'*

'Go,' we say. We are enthusiastic.

'You'll have to do better than that to convince me,' he says.

---

* OUP MP for Fermanagh–South Tyrone constituency, in which Enniskillen lies.

4

More History

In December 1939 Wilfrid Bliss Spender, First Secretary to the Stormont Cabinet, remarked that there was 'one . . . factory in which we could claim that we or the Free State are the largest manufacturers, namely the factory of grievances. I am not at all clear that this is not the most paying one in the Province.'*

Spender's factories of grievance were brought into being by the Government of Ireland Act 1920. The Treaty of the following year between Prime Minister Lloyd George and the Irish established the Free State and took twenty-six of Ireland's counties on the road to independence. Meanwhile, in the remaining six counties, Northern Ireland was created and the British link retained.

II

What people are most likely to know about this state – if they know anything about it at all – is that with Protestants in the majority, Catholics were largely excluded from its social and political structures. Discrimination is often hard to get a handle on, though not in Northern Ireland, where it was openly canvassed, the most notorious example occurring in a widely reported speech of Sir Basil Brooke, later Lord Brookeborough (and Northern Ireland's second prime minister), at

* Brian Barton, *Brookeborough: The Making of a Prime Minister*, p. 151.

an Orange rally at Newtownbutler, Co. Fermanagh, on 12 July 1933. In between an appeal for calm on the part of the Orangemen present and a discussion on agricultural imports (he was the Stormont minister for agriculture at the time), Brooke remarked that

a great number of Protestants ... employed Roman Catholics ... He felt he could speak freely on this subject, as he had not a Roman Catholic about his own place ... He would point out that the Roman Catholics were endeavouring to get in everywhere and were out with all their force and might to destroy the power and constitution of Ulster. There was a definite plot to overpower the vote of Unionists in the north. He would appeal to Loyalists, therefore, wherever possible, to employ Protestant lads and lassies [cheers] ... Roman Catholics ... had got too many appointments for men who were really out to cut their throats if the opportunity arose.*

This speech has become one of the standard reference points whenever the rhetorical question is asked, 'Was there discrimination?' 'Here it is in black and white,' will say those who argue the discrimination case, 'here is a blatant sectarian appeal by the future prime minister of Northern Ireland, in which he insinuates *all* Catholics wish to destroy the state and calls on fellow Protestants not to employ them. Such material to support an argument doesn't come clearer than that, does it?' they will say. The speech is a touchstone for Nationalists and one of the definitive proofs of their case, and if ever there were an Irish *Trivial Pursuit*, I don't doubt identifying Brooke's speech would be an easy point.

* *Fermanagh Times*, 13 July 1933.

Diary

A true story. In a little village on the Tyrone–Fermanagh border, there is only one Lambeg drum. When the Orangemen march on the Twelfth, they take it. When the St Patrick's parade comes round, the Nationalists have their turn with it.

This is in the early 1960s. In 1969, as the Troubles gear up, the arrangement collapses, and each side organizes its own drum, full-time.

5

August 1989

There are two Twelfths in Northern Ireland, which is very confusing for strangers, and they both have origins in the struggle at the end of the seventeenth century between the deposed king, James II, and the man brought in to replace him on the British throne, William of Orange. The first Twelfth, 'The Twelfth' of July, is the day on which William's victory at the Battle of the Boyne in 1690 is celebrated. It was for this that the Scots I met on the ferry from Stranraer were travelling over. Then there is the other Twelfth, of August, on which day is celebrated the success of the Protestants of Derry in withstanding a lengthy Jacobite siege from 18 April to 31 July 1689. The action which started the siege – thirteen apprentice boys seizing the keys and slamming the gates of Derry against the army of James II, who had come to occupy the town – was the inspiration for the establishment of the Apprentice Boys of Derry in 1823.

BANNERS

12 August 1989 was the 300th anniversary of the siege, and in Fermanagh the village scheduled for the marching was Maguiresbridge. It was a day of grey, threatening skies alternating every few minutes with tantalizing glimpses of blue and shafts of sunlight on distant hills.

Outside the village, cars were jammed along the verges, and a handwritten placard hung on a gate into a field:

35

Parking £1.00
Money to the Methodist Church – Repairs

I parked at the top of an alarming slope, beside a car with windows misted by the breaths of the occupants inside.

As I got out, so did they. They were scrubbed men in dark sabbath suits and white shirts. From my car boot, from among the jump leads and old maps, I took my Gore-Tex waterproof. From their boot, from beside two gleaming picnic coolers and a shining car jack, they took brown paper bags. I struggled into my coat. They opened their bags, extracted the collarettes inside (these are popularly known as sashes) and put them on. I found my woollen mittens. They pulled on white gloves and buttoned them. I pulled on my beret. They donned bowler hats and seized neatly rolled umbrellas. I started to amble off. They marched smartly across the grass like city gentlemen. At the gate they turned one way and I the other.

These men were not Orangemen nor Apprentice Boys but Blackmen and members of another Loyal order, the Royal Black Institution or, to use the proper title, the Imperial Grand Black Chapter of the British Commonwealth (and whose day 12 August really is). About half of all Orangemen are in this more exclusive order. You have to be an Orangeman before you are invited to join. Although there are fewer political speeches at its demonstrations, it is just as committed as the Orange Order to Unionism and the defence of Protestantism. It is also associated with the Apprentice Boys of Derry and membership of the two often overlaps.

On the crossroads outside the village, hundreds of people milled around under a black sky. I went over to the stalls at the side of the road. The first sold Union Jacks, some with pictures of the Royal Family on them. The next was crowded with teddy bears and soft cuddly animals made of synthetic fibre.

A group of adolescent girls from a band passed by. They wore uniforms of white blouses and tiny, tight red skirts, with matching red forage caps perched jauntily on their heads. In Ulster eye-liner still reigned supreme, and to a girl their eyelids were either deepest black or richest turquoise.

A few yards away they stopped to talk to some boys, who were wearing blue jackets with gold braid and peaked hats. One was a drummer, and everyone laughed as he used his drumsticks like chopsticks to lift off the hat of a pretty girl. Suddenly the wind howled, and the hat was carried off. The party broke as the girls ran after the hat. The boy called something out, and his girl shouted back. I could not catch the words, but the innuendo was clear, and I kept bumping into more of the same throughout the rest of the day. Marching might be all about 'Protestant triumphalism', as the academics call it, but in my notebook I wrote, 'The day is like Mardi Gras; it is about revelry, licence, misrule, and meeting members of the opposite sex.'

I wandered on through the crowds, admiring the sashes. There was wide variety in colour and length of fringing, and even wider variety in the badges pinned on to them. I noticed the skull-and-crossbones, the seven-pointed star enclosing the cross, Jacob's ladder, the Masons' dividers and set-square, the staff of Hermes, what seemed like a tree (or was it Abraham's bush?) and much more besides. What did it all signify? I had no idea, but what I did sense was that this was the richest example of folk culture I had ever come across in the British Isles, and its mystery was part of its charm.

The village of Maguiresbridge was a collection of low dwellings covered in pebble-dash with grey slate roofs and decorated with Union Jack bunting. I was hoping for a fancy banner, like those I had seen on the way from Larne, with pictures of Protestant heroes and covered with Protestant mottoes. There was a banner, but it was plastic and it read 'Welcome'.

Outside the grey Methodist church the handwritten notice

advertised 'Meat Teas'. A man was collecting money and putting it in an old Crawford's shortbread tin. It was a pound to get in.

Inside the churchyard there was a long trestle table and an outdoor kitchen. For your money you got a paper bag of ham sandwiches and buns and scalding-hot tea. I take mine weak and black, and this so moved the lady who served me, she made the man on the gate give me back fifty pence of my entry money.

'It's not tea, it's scared water he takes,' she said, 'and we can't make him pay for that, can we?'

In the corner there was a canopy with benches underneath, crowded with Blackmen, and another crowd of them were on the other side of the chapel wall in the street, a half bottle of Bushmills slyly passing between them, the whiskey being used to stiffen their tea. Judging by the laughter, the liquor was doing the job.

I went into the chapel where the women and children were. The walls were bare except for a box which showed the hymn numbers. A moment later the lady who had served me outside followed me in.

'You must have some more tea,' she said. 'I've made it especially weak for you. And have a piece of fruit cake,' she added, proffering the plate she had brought. 'Don't say no now – you're too thin. Eat up. I made it myself. And when you've finished, tell me all about yourself. I suppose you've realized we're very nosy in Fermanagh.'

THE PARADE

By one thirty the sun was out. I got myself a good place from which to watch the march, behind the church wall. In the distance I could hear the high-pitched whistle of the piccolos, the clatter of the kettledrums, and the drone of bagpipes.

The bands started to approach, and, as they did, what had

been an incoherent noise gradually clarified into music. The crowd grew more expectant, and spectators at the back began trying to squeeze through to the front. Then, at long last, the procession finally arrived . . .

It was led by James Molyneaux, leader of the OUP at Westminster and the Sovereign Grand Master of the Royal Black Institution.

He was accompanied by four men. One was a cleric, a chain (as opposed to a sash) around his neck. It was a shock to see a man of the cloth in these gaudy circumstances, even though I had known clergymen were often at these parades, because of the Royal Black Institution's commitment to defend the faith.

Behind the leaders came the first Preceptory, a banner between two poles held high above them. This showed (if I remember correctly) a picture in a bold, naïve style of David facing Goliath, and gave the Preceptories' place of origin as Co. Cavan. They were followed by others from the neighbouring Southern border counties of Donegal and Monaghan. I felt a great rush of pride: my country was first. My emotions must have been very confused, for, as I later reflected, the feelings of these men towards the state where they lived were presumably ambiguous.

After the Preceptories from the Republic came their colleagues from Northern Ireland, again each identified by a banner. These were carried by two, sometimes four, strong men, accompanied by young boys who held the tasselled stays and stopped the wind taking off with them. As a further precaution some of the banners were sheathed in plastic.

On every banner there was an image of a Daniel, or a Moses, or an angel, always a doughty solitary fighter from the Protestant past or the Old Testament, executed in that dour Society for the Promotion of Christian Knowledge style which I associate with the books and tracts of Protestant proselytizers of Empire times. In these pictures, it seemed, was evidence of the Protestant 'siege mentality' to which so many commentators on Ireland's Protestants have pointed. This was how they saw themselves, and they had been kind enough to draw it for us. They were defendants of justice, surrounded and outnumbered; but they would fight to the end, and they would win because they were right.

But rather than thinking about this, I was wondering where the Lambegs were. These are the really big drums which men beat until their hands bleed. They have a fearsome reputation, and in Belfast had been and, for all I know, still are banned from marches. The official explanation was that they slowed them down, but it was rumoured the real reason for their restriction to the countryside was their power to arouse aggression.*

After twenty minutes and still no Lambegs, I turned to the man beside me. He had red shiny skin which appeared to be stretched tightly over the bones beneath.

'Right enough, there used to be a man round here who played those,' he told me, 'but he died and no one's taken it up since.' We went on watching for a few moments and then he continued, 'Great skill required to play those Lambegs, you know. You don't just pick one up and bang it. It takes a man years.'

I nodded and it started to hail furiously, the white stones bouncing on the tarmac and landing with a whisper in the grass. In every direction black umbrellas were suddenly raised to the sky. As the musicians played on, the tiny white crystals bounced off the peaks of their hats, and the little sheafs of music clipped to their instruments grew wet and started to sag.

* Dervla Murphy, *A Place Apart*, pp. 287–8.

THE RESOLUTIONS

Then the last of the bands passed, and we heard their music disappearing down the street. Everyone now turned to follow them to 'The Field'.

When they got there, Preceptory members – or Sir Knights as they are called – and spectators gathered round the platform. The meeting started like an AGM. There were welcomes extended, especially to those from across the border, a message was read out from the Provincial Grand Black Chapter of Scotland, and then Sir Knight Molyneaux started reading out the resolutions:

We, the members of the Imperial Grand Black Chapter, reaffirm our devotion and loyalty to the Throne and Person of Her Majesty Queen Elizabeth the Second . . .

The Royal Black Institution reaffirms its loyalty to the essential doctrines of the Reformed Protestant Faith . . .

On behalf of all who care about Ulster and its people, we demand the restoration of stability through reappraisal of the Anglo-Irish Agreement . . .*

In his address, Sir Knight the Revd Robert J. Coulter, Imperial Deputy Grand Chaplain, returned his listeners to a particular moment in the past. He reminded them that they were also celebrating the Battle of Newtownbutler, when the Protestants of Enniskillen had trounced the Catholics of James II. According to the *Impartial Reporter,* he told them to

remember those days 300 years ago when their forefathers were the men who came out from the town of Enniskillen to face the enemy in greater numbers on the field beside Newtownbutler. So great was the consternation among the enemy that they fled from the field of

* *Impartial Reporter,* 17 August 1989.

battle when confronted by the swords and pikes of the men of Enniskillen.

He found the same sort of courage on the field that day . . .*

Here it was again: the 'siege mentality', Protestant triumphalism, and an abnormal connection to the past, dramatized for everyone to see. However, it was hard to hold on to such ideas as I watched the faces of the Blackmen, as they in turn watched the platform with expressions of attention but not of fervour. These were 'rural' faces, with watery blue eyes, cheeks with broken red veins snaking across them, broken ears and crooked teeth stained by tannin and nicotine. The Knights were all trying to look serious, but every time they caught sight of people they knew, the mask slipped as they winked and smiled at them.

After the national anthem I went back to Maguiresbridge, passed under the 'Welcome' banner, which I now noticed had 'Safe Home' written on the reverse side, and made my way back to the Methodist car-park.

ANOTHER VIEW

It had been an extraordinary occasion. I kept trying to think of comparisons as I drove away: the Day of the Dead in Mexico; Corpus Christi in southern Spain; village fiestas I've attended in southern Italy; Croagh Patrick, Co. Mayo, a pilgrimage in which thousands, many in bare feet, struggle to the top of a stony Irish mountain on the last Sunday in July; Maypole dancing at Windsor at Midsummer. It was folk art, if you blanked out the politics part of it.

When I arrived at my next place of call, which was my friend John's house – the one the family had built and moved out to from Enniskillen when he was sixteen – I was still full of it. It was a day out, I enthused, especially for children.

* *Impartial Reporter*, 17 August 1989.

'I wish I'd gone,' said Maureen. She was John's older sister. She was a schoolteacher like he was; she taught in England and was home on her holidays. 'I remember I used to watch from the upstairs window of Aunt Bridie's when I was a child and they marched through the village.'

'Why don't you come next year, then?'

'Why don't I?' she wondered and stared out of the picture window at Cuilcagh Mountain, brown, shaped like a sugar-loaf, impressive by Irish standards at over 2,000 feet, and the landmark along the border between Northern Ireland and the Republic.

Her father – another teacher, a headmaster – nodded in his chair. They were interesting all right, he agreed, but they could also be dangerous. 'Only their own are welcome,' he continued and nodded at Maureen. 'If she'd have gone,' he said, 'they'd have thought she was a spy.'

It was a fun fair where seemingly only half the population were welcome, which left me wondering what, if anything, had been thought about me as I had wandered about, camera and notebook in hand.

LORD BROOKEBOROUGH'S COOK

We went into the dining-room, a big brown cavern at the front of the house and used only for special occasions. I preferred the kitchen, which smelled of marmalade and milk, but this was in my honour, and so I said nothing. The table was laid with the heavy silver cutlery and the best plates, which were white and decorated with shamrocks. There was a turf fire hissing in the grate. The table smelled of wax, and the seats of the chairs were slippery. We ate cold pork with a home-made chutney which had cloves buried in it.

We got on to the subject of the Battle of Newtownbutler, and from there we moved effortlessly to the same town in 1933, and the speech by the future prime minister of Northern

Ireland, Basil Brooke, and his proud boast that he did not have one Catholic working about his place.

'That's not true, of course,' said Mr Maguire, carefully running his knife around the inside of a jar of Heinz salad-dressing.

'Really?'

'His cook was a Catholic. After he made that speech, he probably went home and ate one of her dinners.'

'Are you sure?'

'Sure I'm sure.'

'Could I find her? It was a her, I presume.'

'Yes, it was. I'd have thought it very unlikely, wouldn't you say?'

He looked at Mrs Maguire, who was attempting to unscrew a jar of fresh salad-dressing.

'He might try but I doubt it,' she agreed. Then she said, 'Here, you do it,' and she gave me the jar to unscrew.

Diary

Two weeks after the marching of the Blackmen, it is the Enniskillen Festival. The climax is a parade led by drum majorettes in short red skirts and Quality Street hats, after which the town centre is overrun by buskers and street performers. I am standing near the face-painting stall, watching my daughter turn into a clown, when Mr Holland sidles up and whispers, 'With everyone enjoying themselves, you wouldn't know there's a war on, would you?', then walks away.

After a few hours I leave; this is unfortunate, because, as I learn the next morning, at the end of the evening, in Magee's Spirit House, the crowd sing Nationalist and then Loyalist party songs – 'The Men Behind the Wire' and 'The Sash' – back to back.

On the Monday following I am telephoned by the editor of a Dublin magazine and asked for a piece on Enniskillen. After relating what happened in Magee's, I suggest something about relations in the community.

'*You mean, there were Protestants and Catholics at this thing together?*' says the voice at the other end of the phone.

'*Oh, yes, and they even sang their songs together,*' I say.

Dublin, for the record, is 120 miles away, but for this editor the distance between the two may as well have been a million miles.

6

Lord Brookeborough's Cook

LORD BROOKEBOROUGH

The first Lord Brookeborough was born on 9 June 1888, at Colebrooke House, Co. Fermanagh, the ancestral home, and christened Basil Stanlake Brooke.* The early years of the future prime minister of Northern Ireland were utterly conventional: Winchester, Sandhurst, a commission as a second lieutenant in 1908, and service in India.

In 1912 he followed his father as Grand Master of Hanover Loyal Orange Lodge 1639, the Orange Lodge which served the Colebrooke estate. In the same year he signed the Solemn League and Covenant, declaring his opposition to Home Rule, and was involved in training local members of the Ulster Volunteer Force. This was treason – the intention of

---

* The Brookes were originally English, from Cheshire. The first Brooke in Ireland was an English army captain who commanded a regiment during the conquest of Ulster. He was knighted in 1619 and acquired property in Co. Donegal, of which he became governor. Later he was appointed constable of the castle in Donegal town and given ownership of both it and the town.

His son Henry did equally well. When the Catholics rose in 1641 to throw out the English who had been planted in their midst, he held the town and the castle. In the civil war he wisely chose the Parliamentary side. His loyalty was rewarded with land. He acquired estates at Largie in Co. Fermanagh, the old ancestral home of Lord Maguire. This native clan had dominated Fermanagh for three centuries, but their star was now in descent after the hanging of Lord Maguire at Tyburn.

Henry married twice, producing a Basil by the first wife and a Thomas by the second. The Donegal lands went to Basil, and that line died out. Thomas took Fermanagh, and that line survives.

these forces was to resist the will of the government at West-minster – yet during the First World War the future Lord Brookeborough served loyally on the Western Front and in the Middle East, rising to become ADC to Major General Julian Byng. There has always been, and still is, this kernel of ambiguity in Unionism; it has a tradition of exemplary military service to the Crown and state, yet is prepared to challenge government.

On 3 June 1919, at St George's Chapel, Hanover Square, he married Cynthia Mary Sergison of Cuckfield Park, Sussex, and returned to live at Colebrooke after twenty-five years of absence.

He was county commandant of the Special Constabulary (i.e., the police reserves, with the B-specials comprising the largest component), 1920–23; elected Unionist county councillor in Fermanagh, 1924; chairman of Fermanagh County Council, 1928. He entered Stormont as MP for Lisnaskea, Co. Fermanagh, in 1929; minister for agriculture, 1933–41; minister of commerce and production, 1941–3; prime minister of Northern Ireland, 1943–63. Retired 1968. Died 1973.

Basil was succeeded by Captain John Brooke, who was succeeded by Alan, the third viscount.

*

The first part of a two-volume biography, *Brookeborough: The Making of a Prime Minister* by Brian Barton, was published in 1988, and that is the place to read about the first half of his life. I was more intrigued, however, by what I had been told at the dinner-table; an anti-Catholic speech and then home to a meal cooked by one, which contradicted the very common belief held away from Northern Ireland, that there is no contact whatsoever between the so-called warring parties.

This belief owes its existence to those in the mass media who, unable to find the strength to explain what the place is really like, reach for comparisons which they think will do the work for them: Israel and the occupied territories, Sri Lanka,

Cyprus, the deep South in the United States, Lebanon. This is plain lazy. One could not expect to say – to give a completely off-beat comparison – that biographies of Gielgud and Olivier would be similar, although the subjects are both actors. By the same token it is misleading to imply that different places of conflict have the same qualities. To give one example why this doesn't work: Northern Ireland is a dichotomized society, but there has always been a limited amount of intermarriage, which was not, and is not, the case between blacks and whites in the deep South.

To put it another way, the way I prefer, Northern Ireland has its own characteristics, shared by none of those countries with which it has sometimes been compared, and *these* are what matter. And the cook, if she existed, went to the heart of Northern Ireland's special nature, which is that the two communities, despite the conflict, have also coexisted on the same relatively small piece of ground for 400 years without wiping each other out. This has only been possible, because, despite the antagonistic hyperbole, public utterances have not always been matched by private actions. If Lord Brookeborough did indeed have a Catholic cook at the time he was making his inflammatory speeches, it would illustrate the complex truth that there has always been some mingling of the communities.

For this reason I decided to look for his cook and began asking around.

THE POLICE LEAD

Over the phone he gave me instructions on how to get to his house; I was to go to such and such a village, find such and such a road heading towards such and such a town, count off a number of turnings, proceed to the fifteenth telegraph pole, find the pink garage, fork left 200 yards later, and so on – but his actual postal address he was not prepared to give me.

I arrived and rang the bell. He checked me through the living-room window and then shouted through the closed front door, 'Who is it?'

'What frightens you?' I asked, when we were seated in his living-room.

'You do,' he said, 'and I'll tell you why. In 1982 there was a detective-constable in Enniskillen called Gary Ewing. He was a plain-clothes man. Every week he used to go to the sports centre, the Forum, to do archery. One week, picture in the *Impartial Reporter*, the local paper. 'Gary Ewing,' the caption said, 'enjoying archery.' That was it – no mention of his job. The following week he leaves after his class, gets into his car and bang! He's blown up. Someone had seen that photograph and put two and two together. He was killed with a lovely girl called Helen Woodhouse. She wasn't in the police. She was just unlucky enough to be getting a lift.'

He continued, 'Years ago I'd have done almost everything in uniform. I wouldn't have been frightened to advertise what I was. Not any more. I've been threatened. People have tried to shoot me. I've had bombs. I don't want to die because of some little stupidity. Because my picture's in the paper, or my details are in your book.'

'Well, actually. . .' I said, and explained who I was looking for.

We talked around the subject for a while. He thought the cook might be a Catholic, but the contacts he had out in the village of Brookeborough were long after her time.

Now that it was time to go, he was friendly.

'Don't hesitate now to get in touch,' he said.

'I have your number written down,' I said, 'on a piece of paper but without your name beside it.'

He smiled, 'You're beginning to think like an Ulsterman,' he said.

His last words from the door: 'You know where I am and you know where to find me, don't you?'

I never did find out his address.

THE COOK'S NIECE TWICE REMOVED

The policeman passed me on to my next contact, who told me this story.

'During the campaign in the fifties, an IRA flying column made an attack on an RUC barracks here in Fermanagh and one of the policemen inside the barracks at the time was a relative, a Catholic, of course. He was absolutely terrified when the shooting started, and he didn't manage to fire a single round. The following morning the RUC men had to count up the number of shells they had fired off for their report, and it became obvious my relative hadn't fired a single shot. Nothing was said, but there was the feeling among the other men that he hadn't wanted to fire, because the IRA men were fellow Catholics.'

I steered the conversation back to Lord Brookeborough's cook.

'But don't you see, that's what I'm trying to tell you,' she said.

'I'm sorry?'

'My relative had to leave the RUC and we left the area, so I can't help you. He went to Rhodesia and became a Bush Ranger.'

THE BACHELOR

My next contact was a retired farmer, who lived alone in a big, grey stone house with his housekeeper. He told me this story.

'A Church of Ireland rector went to visit one of his old parishioners. The man kept a loaded shotgun by the door. He explained to the rector that the reason for this was, as he said, "So I can take a shot at them ones, if they come up to the house." The rector was horrified at the idea of keeping a loaded gun by the door in order to take pot-shots at Romans, and he had a long talk with the man, whose name was Bill.

He said, "Bill, you can't be doing things like this. You believe in Jesus Christ our Lord, a man who rather than keep a gun by his door, chose to die on the cross so that men would not keep guns by their doors." Old Bill thought about this for a while, and then he replied, "Well, that's all very well for Jesus Christ, but he didn't have to deal with Roman Catholics."'

I steered the conversation towards my quest. He took off his spectacles and put them on again.

'Sorry.'

A PROFESSIONAL

Within seconds of sitting down in his office, we were on to violence.

'I don't condone killing,' he said, 'but you can understand your man Stone.* When Stone went into Milltown, he thought . . .'

The accountant stopped in mid sentence and stared anxiously towards his door. I turned round in my chair. There was another accountant in the corridor outside, walking towards the twinkling photocopying machine. I knew Mary was a Catholic, which was why, I presumed, the accountant got up and went over and closed the door. It seemed like something from a Victorian novel, where the door is closed to keep the servants from hearing, but this was late August 1989.

'Your man Stone thought,' continued the accountant, quieter than before, "I'll take some of these cunts out, and whoever I get will be guilty", and he was right. All these ones in West Belfast – they may not be in the IRA, but they're helping them. They're all passing information back to the IRA or throwing stones at soldiers.

'We've some round Fermanagh as well. They all vote for Sinn Féin. They're an extremely low class of individual. They're

* A Protestant paramilitary who attacked mourners at a Republican funeral at Milltown Cemetery, West Belfast.

subnormal, in fact. One week they'll be round to the police if their car's stolen, and the next week they'll be trying to kill a policeman. They're bloody hypocrites; all of them getting British Supplementary, the use of the National Health, free education, and all the rest of it, and then they bleat all the time about Brit oppression, Brit torture, Brit misconduct, and the like.'

He couldn't help me with Lord Brookeborough's cook, but he talked like this for hours.

At the door, as he shook my hand when I was leaving, he said, 'You asked me what I voted, didn't you? You won't believe me, I know. SDLP.'

'I'd believe anything,' I said.

THE FIREMAN

'In West Belfast there is a Geordie fireman. When he started, he was told never to open his mouth in West Belfast or to answer any questions at the scene of an incident. This was in case, with his accent and that, he was suspected of being a member of the security forces. If the crowd thought he was, they'd kill him. So, when he went out on fires, and the crowd asked him questions, all he would do was shrug. "Do you know who set the fire, mister?" Shrug. "Was it a bomb, mister?" Shrug. "When'll we get back into our homes, mister?" Shrug. He became so well known, that at all the fires in West Belfast, the crowds starting asking, "Where's the dummy fireman?"'

Another man full of stories, but no help with the woman I was looking for.

A YOUTH

While he went to get a coffee, I glanced at the *Impartial Reporter*. Although it steers a middle course, it is probably perceived as a Protestant paper, as distinct from the local Catholic paper, the *Fermanagh Herald*.

'What does this mean?' I asked when he sat down, reading from the box advertisement which had intrigued me. 'Wanted, Christian girl to share flat.'

He looked at me across the Formica table.

'Does that mean they want a Protestant?' I said.

'No, no,' he said finally, quite firmly. 'It doesn't mean they want a Protestant. Christian means someone very religious. I mean, a very heavy Roman Catholic wouldn't be a Christian.'

I didn't even bother asking about the cook.

The next week he went off to start his training with the Royal Air Force.

MOTHER AND DAUGHTER

'The week after the bomb went off here at the war memorial, it was awful,' said the mother. 'We were like people rushing to comfort each other after an air raid. I had this awful sense of guilt. Somehow I was to blame, because I was a Catholic. Now, mind you, I don't think the children in the town felt that. I don't think mine felt that. It was just an irritation to them. Something that was getting in the way of everything. Wouldn't you say, Mary?'

Her fifteen-year-old daughter was sitting on the sofa, reading an article about the Pet Shop Boys in a magazine.

'Well, yous was embarrassed with your Protestant friend, like,' she agreed.

'Do you remember feeling anything after the bomb?' her mother persisted.

'No.'

'Nothing? Nothing whatsoever?'

'It was like you said. It got in the way.'

The attitude was fascinating, but they were no help with my quest.

THE HEADMASTER

'There's a glass curtain here,' he said. 'When you first arrive, you can't see it, and many people who live here can't see it either, or won't. But it's here all right, separating the two communities, only you don't find out about it until you walk into it – bang! – and break your nose.'

Riveting but no help on the cook front.

YOUNG LORD BROOKEBOROUGH

Driving towards Colebrooke, the Brookeborough family seat in south Fermanagh, on the afternoon of my appointment with the third viscount and grandson of the old man, I asked myself why I hadn't started my search for the cook with him.

Squeamishness, was the answer. The next hour could well be tricky. No doubt the man had probably had to put up with hundreds of inquiries about his grandfather's 1933 speeches, since they were what was best known about him. I was going to be up against the boredom factor. There was also the sensitivity problem. What descendant in his right mind was going to welcome a twerp into his house for tea, whose thesis was that his grandfather, rather than being an exceptional bigot, was in fact just a plain old run-of-the-mill hypocrite? None that I could imagine.

I found myself in a maze of tiny lanes with high hedgerows. I passed an enormous set of gates. They were austere, even grim. They were also abandoned and chained shut. On the other side of the road there was a long, low Neo-Classical structure, like an outbuilding from the Kensal Green Crematorium, which I later discovered was the old estate school. I was in the vicinity of Colebrooke all right, but I peered in vain to left and right for a fleeting sight of a grey 'Great House'. I was well and truly lost.

An old man working in his garden finally put me right: I had been circling the estate. With a couple of quick lefts I was in. Suddenly I found myself in flat parkland, with sloping hillsides in the distance which sheered like railway cuttings. A red deer was nibbling at the grass.

I had come in by the back route and approached the main house via the outbuildings. These were a medley of old stone structures brought into the twentieth century by the addition of corrugated tin roofs and galvanized gates. Long grass grew around the edges of the yards, and here and there lay pieces of abandoned machinery. The days when the estate had been large and profitable seemed long gone.*

The road turned, and the gardens with flowerbeds, lawns and fine old trees sprang into view. The house was next: a grey, austere, imposing building. I parked and got out. There was silence except for an eerie shriek which sounded distinctly like a peacock's cry. No one about, I thought. Then a man appeared around the side of one of the parked cars. There was a look of anxiety on his face. Not social anxiety but the real McCoy – just like I had seen on the policeman's face. A few yards behind him, I noticed now for the first time, was a line of poles with searchlights which ringed the house.

I hurriedly explained to the third viscount who I was. Real anxiety now turned back into its social equivalent. His hand went up to his head. 'Oh, my goodness gracious.' He had not only completely forgotten I was coming, but he was now in the middle of doing something with the sheep which could not be broken off.

Together we sprinted back through the gardens, carrying cans of Courage beer for the farmhands. We found them in a corral, chasing hundreds of sheep backwards and forwards. The air was filled with the cries of the animals and the patter of their feet on the ground.

* In 1876 the estate amounted to 28,000 acres. It was the third largest in Fermanagh.

Back at the house again, having handed out the beers, we sat down opposite one another at the wrought-iron table on the patio.

'I've only got a few minutes,' he said.

I had looked at photographs of the old man, and now here was a chance to study the descendant. They were clearly from the same stock – the family resemblance was especially clear about the eyes – but the expression with which the two viewed the world was utterly different. The old man's gaze was imperious and, to my mind, had a threatening cast to it in the 'Don't mess with me or you'll regret it' vein. Two generations later that had given way to something much more benign and far less defensive. A sign, I thought, of how much things have changed.

'Now, how exactly can I help you?' he asked, breaking a ginger-snap.

I knew exactly. The problem was, how did I broach a subject in ten seconds when I had banked on having forty-five minutes to work my way round to it?

'It's a lovely situation here,' I said.

Small talk ebbed and flowed. In my mind's eye I could see an egg-timer with the sands running through it.

His wife appeared. The sands trickled on.

The current viscount drained his tea-cup and glanced across the garden in the direction of the outbuildings. Any moment now he was going to stand, apologize and leave; my chance would be gone.

'I wanted to ask you something about your grandfather,' I said, 'and the speeches of, ah, 1933, when . . .'

A rapid nod and a faintly glazed expression told me I was following where hundreds had gone before.

'I was told that in fact he did employ Catholics.'

'I wouldn't have thought so,' he said.

'Highly unlikely,' added his wife.

They both shook their heads.

'Just before my grandfather made those speeches,' said his

grandson, 'the IRA threatened to kidnap a young child here. It's not often discussed, and because of that I wouldn't have thought therefore . . .'

His voice trailed off. He assumed I knew what he was talking about. I did not, and a moment later, after he had stood up, said goodbye and bounded off, I asked his wife.

'The child was Julian – Alan's uncle – he was killed in the war. It was a sort of matter of honour with the IRA, I believe, to get him. This might have been the reason for the speeches, and it was certainly a reason why there wouldn't have been any Roman Catholics here, I would have thought. But do ask Alan's mother.'

Peacocks came from the garden and started to strut around the table.

'Their rate of reproduction is something extraordinary,' she said. 'Alas, you can't take their eggs away, because the wretched things just start again. So what I do – it's a bit cruel – I boil the eggs and then leave the mother nesting on them until her fertile time is over.'

There was a shriek, and a male began to shimmy and shiver and fan his gorgeous tail at a female.

'See what I mean. At it again,' she laughed.

I left, as I had come in, by the back route. In the yard there was no sign of the farmhands. I presumed they were in the shed, drinking beer with the viscount.

In the park the deer I had passed on the way in ran along beside the car before bounding away into the trees.

*

It had been a good idea to look for the cook, but it was more than likely she did not exist. She was an apocryphal truth rather than a literal one. Besides which – although this wouldn't stop me asking around for her – I now had the idea of the Glass Curtain, and that seemed like a much better anchor.

I had been around for only a few weeks, and yet it did feel to me as if there were a Glass Curtain in Northern Ireland, an invisible divide between the communities that mirrored the more obvious one several hundred miles to the east, but was at the same time very different from that one. What I would attempt in the year ahead would be to describe it and to record some moments of collision with it.

There was also a nice tie-in. The idea of the Glass Curtain derived from the Iron Curtain, which was Churchill's phrase,* and it was he who had coined the phrase about 'the dreary steeples of Fermanagh'.

And all this tied in with something even bigger going on in Europe. The day I had seen the headmaster something extraordinary had happened. In Poland two old partners of the Communist Party – the Peasants and the Democratic Parties – had switched to Solidarity, and early that day the Polish parliament had elected Tadeusz Mazowiecki, the first ever non-Communist prime minister in the Eastern bloc since the late forties.

Change was in the air, but was Poland, always a maverick, a marker for the future or a one-off? Was the Iron Curtain going to stay or go, and would this say anything about Ireland? These were interesting times.

Diary

I go to a friend's for dinner. There is talk about the Greens.† Could they be the party to unite both sides? After all, acid rain fell on the fields of Nationalist and Unionist alike.

'I hate to sound a sour note,' says one of the guests with mild irony, 'but before they make any more headway, you know, they will have to state their position on the border.'

* 'From Stettin in the Baltic to Trieste in the Adriatic, an iron curtain has descended across the Continent' (Churchill speaking at Westminster College, Fulton, Missouri, 5 March 1946).
† In the 1987 general election, the Greens (known then as the Ecology Party) had scored 281 votes. In the 1989 European parliament election, I understand their vote rose to 6,000.

7
An Old Unionist

GEORGE ARTHUR CATHCART

Bellanaleck is a small village four miles outside Enniskillen. There is a post office-cum-general shop and opposite stands a long, low building with a thatched roof and a stable door. Once the old post office, it is now a restaurant and one of Northern Ireland's few entries in the *Good Food Guide*. The proprietors of both are the Cathcarts, and I had come to see the patriarch of the family, George.

A woman, a waitress from the restaurant, showed me into the parlour of the house, and I found him waiting in front of a fire. He was a big elderly man, in a suit and tie and spectacles.

'Shall I serve the tea?' the woman asked. She was slight and quiet with a whispering voice, and, unless my ears deceived me, she called him 'Boss'.

There is a curious reassurance when events develop as you expect. Yes, I thought, sinking on to the sofa, as the woman clattered about with the tea things in the corridor outside, this is how it ought to be with an old-style Unionist; a roaring fire, a genial chat and a good woman bringing refreshments.

*

'There was going to be a meeting held in Arney,' he said, 'which was mainly a Roman Catholic place, about establishing a branch of the [Ulster] Farmers' Union. It was mainly Catholics who went, along with a few Protestants, one of whom was this man called Connor, who hadn't much religion and I think was a bit of an atheist.

59

'Anyhow, they're having this meeting and the canon was up on stage along with the speaker sent down by the Farmers' Union, a man called Humphrey Jameson. He explained to them what the rules and regulations of the Farmers' Union were and everything they needed to know. Then this man Connor stood up and he said, "Can I ask Mr Jameson a question?" "Yes, you can," said the canon. "Would Mr Jameson agree," said Connor, "that the Department of Agriculture gives money to the Farmers' Union?" Humphrey Jameson rather reluctantly had to admit that this was true. When the thing was set up in 1917 and struggling, the government had agreed to give them £1,000 a year, which was a lot of money in those days. "So how can you ask us to form a branch to fight them," says Connor, "when you're in their pocket?" So there was no branch of the union formed there.

'The organizer of the meeting, Pat Cox, was very disappointed, and so he came to me and he said, "Shall we try it in Bellanaleck?" I said, "Why not give it a try?" The big question was then where would we hold this meeting. If it was in the Orange Hall, would the Catholics come? And if it was going to be in the Catholic Hall, would the Protestants go? We agreed on a compromise. We held the meeting in my cow shed. It was a great success; we had half from one side of the house, half from the other, and we formed a branch.'

Membership of the union led to an invitation to join the Milk Marketing Board, of which he became vice-chairman. Simultaneously George Cathcart rose to become president of the union, representing Northern Ireland in the annual February price reviews at Whitehall. He was also a member of the Northern Ireland Fire Authority, for his services to which he was awarded the OBE.

Meanwhile, in tandem with the rise in his level of public service, there was political ascent. The ward of Corryglass, near Letterbreen, had a vacancy. He was proposed for the ward and accepted.

'Once you'd been accepted in those days,' he explained, 'as the Unionist candidate, there was no election – the Nationalists wouldn't contest the seat, and no one on your side stood against you – and so you went automatically on to the borough council.'

'Are you still a councillor?' I asked.

He stirred the milk in his tea and muttered something about later leaving politics.

'It was under something of a cloud,' he added, and then he told me about something he had done which had been regarded as pro-Nationalist.

I picked up my pencil and started writing in my notebook.

'You can't write about that,' he said.

'Oh.'

'No,' he said and shook his head. He preferred to leave the subject alone. If I wrote about it, that would only stir up old animosities and reopen old wounds. 'So don't quote me,' he said, and the conversation turned to the day he had gone to Buckingham Palace to receive his OBE.

AFTERWARDS

Driving away, I had a salutary talk with myself. I had not stumbled, as I had thought, on an old-style Unionist. I had found something even rarer: a rebellious one. I liked the idea, because it was an antidote to the stereotypical view of *all* Northern Ireland folk as inflexible.

But I had failed to get the story – a particular talent I have – and I rebuked myself for not having done some research before the meeting, gone primed with the knowledge of the commendable thing George Cathcart had done, and had some convincing arguments up my sleeve as to why he ought to allow me to repeat it.

Diary

A story.

In years gone by there is, in Enniskillen, a highly respected man. He is a non-practising member of the Church of Ireland who makes it a point of principle never to take sides.

The man dies, and his son takes over the family business. One day a stalwart of the local Orange Lodge comes in and says, 'I've come to take back your father's sash.'

'But my father never was a member of the Lodge,' says the son.

'He was,' says the stranger, and he gives instructions to go and look in a particular drawer in a particular desk at the back of the office.

The son goes through and opens the drawer and there, indeed, is the sash.

After he returns it, he wonders why, through all the years, his father had never told him.

8

An Old Nationalist

JIM LUNNY

After leaving George Cathcart's, I went immediately to Cornagrade, a housing estate outside Enniskillen, to see Jim Lunny, a lifelong Nationalist now in his eighties and still an active member of the council.

I found his house and rang the bell. A few moments later the door opened. I saw an elderly, square man with an unblinking stare. There was a rasp to his voice as he spoke. (Cigars, I later discovered.)

He brought me through to the living-room and apologized for the untidiness. He was a widower, he explained. It was a long, narrow room with heavy curtains, a fire burning in the grate, and prominent on the wall a large framed colour photograph of Senator Edward Kennedy and the leader of the SDLP, John Hume. They were posed standing in front of the Irish tricolour, and their autographs were at the bottom. (Later I got a closer look. Kennedy's writing was large and flamboyant, Hume's small and punctilious. Kennedy had written 'Congratulations on your election' in big looping curves, while Hume had written simply 'Well done', which seemed to say everything which needs to be said about the difference between the Old World and the New. I assumed the election in question was Lunny's.)

We settled by the fire. 'What was your childhood like?' I asked.

'I grew up with the boys from what I call the "Latin Quarter",' he began, 'the most poor and deprived part of the town. A lot of the parents of the boys I knocked around with went off to the 1914–18 war, and then they came back to Fermanagh and they couldn't get anything. There was terrible poverty then. I was educated by the Presentation Brothers in the St Michael's Reading Rooms where we had this tragedy – '

'You mean the war memorial bomb?' I interrupted.

'Yes, where they put the bomb – that was my school. I well remember the day, several of us were climbing up the gate or something, when the war memorial, which was opposite, was first unveiled with the Union Jack fluttering over it. We saw all these people gathered around it, and they were ones who hadn't spent an hour of their life in the army.

'After they all went off, we went over and we saw the names on the side and they were Catholic names, but none of their relatives had been at this inauguration ceremony. Oh, no. That was my first inkling of the two groups – the "white colony" and the "Latin Quarter". They were the rulers and we were the natives.'

Lunny's father worked in an egg and poultry business owned by a man called Smith. He was the storeman. After school Lunny junior was lucky to get a job with the Enniskillen Electric Light Company.

'At the end of my first week, I was on the floor, filing letters in cardboard boxes (we had no filing cabinets), when the owner came in and said, "Aren't you a Methodist?" "Oh, no, I'm a Catholic," I said. "Oh! I thought you were a Methodist," he said. He thought that because Smith, my father's employer, was a Methodist. It was like that in those days.

'In the sixties sometime, I can't remember exactly when, I was elected to the old borough council. Just to give you the flavour of the place, there was a Unionist called Eddie Elliott, and at meetings he would bash his cane on the table and pronounce, "We're not going to cut a stick to beat ourselves with," which I understood to mean he opposed building houses for Catholics because he believed at elections they would vote against the Unionists.

'Housing was a big thing. I remember one time, we had

forty of these new aluminium houses, and eight Catholics had been put forward for them. At the end of the day, however, only two Catholics were successful. But what made it worse, one of these new homes went to Councillor — if you can believe it. He was a Protestant. He came from the South. He was probably intimidated out of there in the twenties by the IRA and came North.

'To backtrack a moment, sometime before all this Councillor — had come to me and said that he had been offered a good house in Enniskillen to buy but he didn't have the money and what did I think of this. I said to him that he had to go to the bank because he had a good wage, and that he had to buy that house. Which he did, but then he sold that house, just before he was allocated the aluminium house.

'After the meeting I remember one of the Unionists saying to me, "Don't blame Councillor —. Blame X, he's the one who talked Councillor — into it." That's the thing with Unionists, they're awful honest in private, but when it comes to the vote, they follow the party line blindly. Anyway, I was so fired up by the whole thing I left the council. Then the SDLP was formed and I joined them.'

'But things are better now, are they not?' I pressed him.

'When I joined the Western Area Library and Education Board in 1973,' he said, 'I looked at what we call the "top table", and I saw that with one exception they were all Protestants. This is the first thing you look for. You're bred to it. And in the sixteen years I was on the board the officers changed, so that by the end it was fifty-fifty.'

'So things are better.'

He gave a big smile. 'Our problem is that we still have to contend not only with the Catholic Sinn Féiners but also with the Protestant Sinn Féiners.'

'And who are they?' I wondered.

'I'd include under that heading the OUP and the DUP. Just to backtrack again to the days of old Elliott, the one with the stick, when he was chairman, the split on the council then was fifty–fifty between Unionist and Nationalist. George Cathcart – do you know who I mean?'

I nodded, my interest rising, without mentioning I had just come from talking to him.

'And Francis Gage wanted the chair to rotate; Unionists would have it one year, Nationalists the next. It was common sense. They wanted Tom Daly to be the chairman for a year and he a Nationalist. And when the vote came, they supported Daly and he was elected.'*

'Can I write about this?' I asked.

'Why wouldn't you?' Jim Lunny replied, and then he continued, 'At the next election, George Cathcart had his nomination withdrawn and was slaughtered. Gage was squeezed out as well. Any lenient Unionist was always forced out by the party. But my point is, the problems of today were created all those years ago. At the time we had this terrible tragedy in the town . . .'

'The bombing,' I interrupted again.

'Yes, we had eight Sinn Féin councillors. And they were using the same tactics the Unionists had used before. They were making certain there was a Nationalist majority on every committee. You'd think the Sinn Féiners would look back at sixty years of Unionist misrule and think, "Are we going to do what the Unionists did to us?" You'd think that's what they'd think, but they don't think, do they! And then that Sinn Féin chairman wouldn't even condemn the bombing. In consequence they went four down in the next election, giving us twelve Unionists to eleven Nationalists.'

'And you still aspire to a United Ireland?'

'I do. My vision is a funny one, but I believe we're all Irish. We had this party of Conservative MPs in Enniskillen some time ago, and Sammy Foster – he's Official Unionist – and some others of the same persuasion were talking to them and they were saying "we this" and "we that", and I listened for a

* *Impartial Reporter*, 5 June 1975.

while, and then I interrupted and I said, "I don't belong to the royal 'we'. I'm a Republican." Sammy Foster looked at me, he was outraged, and he said, "You're SDLP." I said, "That's right, but we're Republicans, only we won't shoot anyone to get what we want. Why don't you join with us and then we can all have an Ireland together in which we're all equal and in which we all have an equal share?"'

Jim Lunny went out to the kitchen and came back with a tray of drinks. 'My hobby is drinking Guinness,' he said. 'I drink the wine of the country.'

'Do you honestly believe that yourself and Sammy Foster, Unionists and the SDLP, could join together?' I asked.

'If I was the same age as you, I'd say – yes.'

AFTERWARDS

Walking back to the car, I paused at the end of the street and looked across the waters of the Erne to the island of Enniskillen and the RUC barracks lit up by searchlights, its radio antennae like feelers and its blast-proof cladding like a carapace. In effect it was a military fort, with the town lying behind dominated by the two churches on the hill. With the exception of a single car with its headlamps on, sweeping along Queen Elizabeth Road, there was not a sign of life in the streets, although it was only ten o'clock.

Looking down on the deserted town reminded me of a conversation I had had a day or two earlier with an old Enniskillener I had met in a pub. 'Before '69 the town at night was crawling with people,' he said, 'all the towns in Northern Ireland were, and then this thing started and everyone went in home and they locked their doors and they haven't come out since.'

Judging by what I was now seeing, this appeared to be true, and despite the brave thing George Cathcart had done, the population were still at home in their bunkers.

Diary

On Boa Island, on Lower Lough Erne, I am told there are Janiform – two-faced, Janus-like – figures, the subject of one of Seamus Heaney's verses, and that they are worth a visit. So one afternoon I go off in search of them with an Australian friend, Jason, who has come to stay.

The way to the graveyard is along a private concrete road. But the farmer whose land is on either side has erected a makeshift fence out of sheep wire at the top. We roll back the fence, drive to the end and find ourselves in a farmyard. There is a silage pit covered with black plastic and old perished tyres. The outhouses are like pillboxes.

An old paling with some missing rungs surrounds the graveyard. We undo the blue baling twine which holds the swing gate shut, and we go in. Among the clumps of hedge and the long grass we can make out a couple of gravestones tilting at alarming angles. The Janiform figures stand in the middle. They have been set in concrete by some custodian of ancient monuments. They are very old, two-faced figures, with huge pointed chins and staring eyes.

We stand in front of them, and they stare back at us. I am impressed now, but I know the real effect of the figures will not show until later, when I discover that I can close my eyes and picture them perfectly, without having made any effort to memorize the pieces at this time.

We go back to the agri-business car-park, and Jason says, 'Anywhere else in the world, there'd be a café and a bureau de change at a site like this.'

PART TWO

AUTUMN

9

The Trick Cyclist

THE HOSPITAL

It was autumn in Belfast, the gutters strewn with leaves.

I went to see a psychiatrist. He was a nice man. I saw him in his office, a tiny, sweaty box with a humming fluorescent light. He smoked, which I always take to be a good sign in a medical man.

'How does everyone here cope?' I asked.

'They just get on with living and doing what has to be done,' he said, 'and they accept the fact that they might die violently as a perfectly normal part of everyday life.'

This was underpinned by the widespread belief that the problem with the problem was that it could *never* be solved. Once you had this on board, he said, you could accept you might die a violent death.

Now this was an admirable mechanism for allowing life to continue under difficult circumstances, I thought, as I made my way out along corridors smelling of pee and cabbage. The problem was, if you did not believe the Troubles could ever be resolved, any aspirations or hopes or dreams for a better future were unsustainable.

RESEARCH

The psychiatrist gave me a number of papers to read on the subject of conflict and psychological well-being, with titles like 'The Psychopathology of Civil Disorder' and 'Psychiatric Aspects of Terrorist Violence: Northern Ireland 1969–1987'.

Reading through the latter paper, I found my interest caught by the last section, entitled 'Cohesion'. In New Haven, Connecticut, in 1975, a group of 938 people who had been part of a community survey of mental health the previous year provided a unique opportunity to test the psychological effects of violence; of mixed ethnic and racial background, they had experienced a series of severe riots in the city's black sector which had left the adjacent white areas untouched. White males in the survey, it was found, felt significantly better during and after the rioting, while white females felt no different during but significantly better afterwards. Among the whole population, black, white, male and female, none felt worse, and in fact black women felt better during the rioting.*

The uncomfortable conclusion that rioting is not necessarily bad and may even contribute to psychological well-being is one with which several commentators in the United States would agree. R.M. Fogelson, for instance, reflecting in 1970 on the black riots during the previous decade, noted during them 'the outpouring of fellow feeling, of mutual respect and common concern . . . camaraderie . . . carnival spirit . . . exhilaration so intense as to border on jubilation . . . a sense of pride, purpose and accomplishment . . . their common predicament revealed in the rioting, blacks looked again at one another and saw only brothers'.†

The United States is not Northern Ireland. On the other hand, what the evidence from there points up is that perhaps there is a *balance* of effects when you have civil disorder, as opposed to there just being bad effects, as one would assume. If this is the case, then that would explain why psychological well-being in Northern Ireland (measured in terms of suicides, para-suicides, prescriptions of sleeping tablets, and so on) is about the same as anywhere else in the United Kingdom. Some

* P.S. Curran, 'Psychiatric Aspects of Terrorist Violence: Northern Ireland 1969–1987', *British Journal of Psychiatry* (1988), no. 153, p. 474.
† ibid.

people are distressed by what happens to them (especially if they directly experience violence), but others are exhilarated by it. The Troubles make them feel better, which may be yet one more reason for the unsolvable nature of the problem.

Diary

At the fag end of the party, when the ashtrays are being emptied and the coffee is being made to sober up the last guests before we set off for home, I talk to Sara, early twenties, pretty.

'If you believed what you read in the papers,' she said, 'you'd think civil war was raging everywhere in Northern Ireland. But if you live here, and you think of trouble, you think of it as happening in certain towns. And if you live in those certain towns, you think of it as happening in certain districts. And if you live in those certain districts, you think of it as happening on certain housing estates. And if you live on those certain housing estates, you think of it as happening in certain streets. And if you live in those certain streets, you know that the trouble is being caused by the man at the end of the road in the house with the blue door.'

10

September

THE SYSTEM

In Northern Ireland there are two kinds of school, just like there are two kinds of everything else. 'Maintained' schools are Catholic, and 'controlled' schools are Protestant. They deliver the same syllabus and are to all intents and purposes identical, except that maintained schools receive 85 per cent of their capital costs against the 100 per cent received by the controlled schools.* The only difference is in the religion of the pupils who attend.

To suggest that the separation between children of the two religions is absolute is to exaggerate. Over the last twenty years many schools, acting in a conciliatory spirit, have formed relationships with schools of opposite faith. However, while recognizing what an advance this is, one must not be fooled into thinking that here is a pointer for the future. It is not friends today, one school for all tomorrow. These 'relationships' are concessions ultimately designed to prevent what both educational establishments do not want: all children going to one type of school. There is an unspoken understanding between them – including those elements who are hostile to any kind of local *rapprochement* – that the *status quo* must and will continue.

---

* Sports are different, with Gaelic Athletic Association sports being the norm in the boys', maintained schools, rugby and soccer in the boys' controlled and voluntary grammar schools. There is a similar split in the girls' sector, camogie (girls' hurling) being the norm in the former and hockey in the latter. There have also been wide differences in the history taught in Catholic and Protestant schools, but these are no longer so significant.

And what are the consequences of separate education? A Catholic friend told me that at her convent school, they believed Protestant girls were given contraceptives by their school nurses. When she got to university, she found out it was not so. In my experience funny ideas among Protestants about Catholics are similarly numerous.

Does separate education have a dark side? Is it easier to accept the tit-for-tat killing of one of 'them', if you haven't gone to school with any of 'them', and if you have then gone on to work and live in places where you don't meet any of 'them' either? Any answer must be speculative. Maybe mixed schooling would make no difference at all, but it cannot be healthy to grow up in ignorance.

THE INTEGRATED SCHOOL

John Maxwell was sitting at home outside Enniskillen, when the bomb went off at the war memorial. He heard about it on the radio, although he lives only a few miles outside the town.

His background is Protestant. He was educated at Portora Royal when it was a public school. He takes his holidays in Mullaghmore, a village by the sea in Co. Sligo, just across the border. Lord Mountbatten and his family (who owned Classiebawn, the 'Great House') once took their holidays regularly there as well.

John Maxwell had one son, Paul. He was befriended by the Mountbattens and often sailed with them. On 27 August 1979 the IRA placed a bomb on Mountbatten's boat. It was then detonated by remote control by somebody standing on the mainland, just after the boat had put out to sea from Mullaghmore harbour. Mountbatten was killed, along with his grandson Nicholas and Paul Maxwell (with Mountbatten's daughter's mother-in-law, Doreen Lady Brabourne, dying subsequently of injuries). John Maxwell was standing in the harbour when the bomb went off.

'My initial reaction,' said John Maxwell in a very quiet voice when we reached this point in his account, 'was one of extreme anger which lasted, I suppose, about five minutes.'

'Vengeful, do you mean?'

'Not so much that, really,' he said, 'it was just an anger that it had happened, and that Paul, who was as much Irish as anyone else on this island, and who'd been brought up to be a liberal youngster, had been killed. If the aim is a United Ireland, why kill the people you want to bring with you into it? It seemed so ridiculous. I remember thinking that at the time.

'When I found his body, I wrapped it up with the help of a friend. I can remember feeling very angry and shouting at people. And then that just went, just like that, and I've never felt it since.

'But when it went, I thought, no one should ever feel like this. No one should ever feel this complete and utter desolation. Then I can clearly remember thinking, this killing has got to stop. I realized right then that I was going to have to do something. And something to do with education was always in the back of my mind from that moment on.'

After the funeral he returned to Fermanagh College, where he was a lecturer in sociology. I asked him how he coped, being back at work so soon after. He did not know, he told me. I would have to ask his colleagues.

I asked if he had felt disengaged.

'Yes – particularly at the start.'

'How did the world seem to you?'

'I remember saying to myself, look, it's important you go through the motions, because I'd read that somewhere, and I knew that if I did, things would eventually come right. And that's what I did. But the things I was doing did not seem important to me, whereas before they would have. This was particularly true in my job. Where before I would have got annoyed or irritated or delighted about what was going on in the college, now I didn't care any more.'

He began to suffer from migraines that lasted for hours. They were brought on by dreams of Paul, particularly of the body after he had found it, or by talking about what happened, or by thinking about it.

Eight years later came the bomb at the Enniskillen war memorial, which acted as a catalyst in Maxwell's mind. With others he began work on setting up an integrated primary school. The previous ten years had seen the appearance of a handful of such schools, attended by children of all faiths, where Christian instruction was determined by the wishes of the parents. All these had been in Belfast or its environs. The Enniskillen school would be the first in the west. As the work got underway, the migraines almost disappeared.

'Was there any hostility,' I asked, 'when it became clear what you were doing?'

'Worse than that,' he replied. 'Every so often the kids at the college get fed up. They want half a day off, so they phone up and say there's a bomb in the place.

'Anyway, one day this happened, and we were all standing outside the college waiting for the building to be searched. An old lady was standing beside me – I suppose she'd be about sixty – I'd seen her before but I'd never talked to her. I'd formed the impression she was a very quiet woman who never said boo to a goose.

'All of a sudden I was aware of her shouting, and I wondered what she was shouting about. Then I turned round and found she was shouting at me. I was amazed. I said, "Are you talking to me?" "Of course I'm talking to you," she said. "It's your fault, all these bombs." I said, "Hold on a minute. What are you talking about?" "This integrated school," she said. "We have to stand together as Protestants, you know, and not be doing things like *that*." "Listen," I said, "we're just trying to improve the situation." But she wouldn't be convinced. She was almost hysterical. And it was very embarrassing, because the whole staff were standing there, listening.'

*

There was a meeting for parents a week before the integrated school opened its doors. When the chair mentioned a sash that was going to be part of the school uniform, a man in the audience grew very agitated.

'What's this about the sash, then?' he said. He was English and recently settled in Enniskillen. 'I thought up here the sash was a bit, you know . . .'

'Oh no,' said the chair, 'it's not *that* sort of sash. It's just a nice wee belt to go round the girls' tunics, to set them off.'

He was greatly relieved.

The day the school opened was a grey one. We drove my daughter in. She was wearing her new uniform but no sash. We had forgotten to buy one.

The site of the school is on the edge of Enniskillen. It consists of an asphalt playground and three Portakabins.* The media were everywhere, so many in fact that I wondered if they outnumbered parents and children.

The school had not received a penny of government cash. The money had either come from private charitable trusts or been provided by the parents themselves through various fund-raising activities. State support would only start once the school had demonstrated there was a demand in the community for the kind of education it supplied, and that would not be judged for eighteen months or even two years. Meanwhile, the school was going to be free just like a state school and was open to anyone, although obviously a balance of Protestants and Catholics would be maintained.

A few tears were shed by the organizers; they had achieved some feat in getting a school up and running. In the yard the children played, making their unmistakable playground roar, while parents drank coffee in the office and watched the news crews.

* The school now has a permanent hall and offices, and there are plans for permanent classrooms.

78

Before the bell I went over to India's classroom. It was filled with pictures, vases of flowers and old-style sloping desks which had been newly painted blue. I left her Snoopy pencil case for her, and we got into the car. Driving home, I remembered the psychiatrist and our conversation; the problem with the problem was that it could never be solved, and once you accepted that, you could live quite happily in Northern Ireland. All it cost you were your hopes for the future. The school was a direct contradiction of that.

Diary

On Boa Island, in Lower Lough Erne, there is a permanent VCP. It should be at the border at Pettigoe (a few miles further north), but since there it would be in danger of mortar attack from the Republic, it is here instead.

'Where did you live in London?' asks the soldier scrutinizing my wife's driving licence after we pull in.

'Kensington.'

'Oh, yeah. I've been down Kensington. Posh.'

'No, not that Kensington. North Kensington. Wormwood Scrubs, really. Very different.'

'Not as good as Sheffield, though.'

'That where you're from?'

'Magic place. Going back in a month. This is my second tour of duty here.'

'How do you like it?'

He looks heavenward.

'You on holiday?' he asks.

'No, we're living here.'

'Down South. That's all right, innit?'

'No, up here.'

'What! Living in Northern Ireland? You must be mad.'

'It's a lovely place, really.'

'*I'm going back to Sheffield in a month.*' *He looks heavenward again.* '*I won't detain you. There's another car waiting.*'

On the other side of Boa Island, Tyga and I have two choices: left and on to Belleek or right – the old road to Pettigoe, now described as '*Closed because Cratered*'. *We go right.*

We find ourselves on a lovely road with distant views of cottages. Everywhere are fields of green pastures and trees with hanging branches which touch our car roof. The countryside closest to the border is probably the best preserved in Northern Ireland.

We pass an abandoned chapel and go under the railway bridge which once carried the train from Enniskillen to Bundoran, and further on stumble upon a huge mansion with cows wandering over the lawn. There is a lightbulb burning in a back kitchen and someone moving inside.

A few moments later she appears. She sounds mittel-*European. I wonder what she is doing here but don't ask. I huddle over my map instead. We are just in the North, she explains, and the river I can glimpse beyond the trees is the border.*

'*There was a bridge across,*' *she confirms,* '*but the Garda blew it up. They couldn't keep watching it any more.*'

If we go back, she tells me, and turn down the first track, we will find a ford at the end right beside the blown-up bridge. The locals use this ford all the time, but she does not recommend it. If we are caught, we will be turned back with a caution by the Garda, or we might be fined, or the car might even be impounded.

Five minutes later we are fording the river by the blown-up bridge. Our hearts are thumping, it has to be admitted, but more because we fear getting stuck in the swiftly moving waters than because we fear getting caught.

On the other side there is a field, and at the end we go through a gate and find ourselves on the road to Pettigoe.

Coming into the village a mile later, I am reminded of crossing the border from the United States into Mexico. The earth, air and vegetation are the same both where you were and where you are, but obligingly Mexico feels new and different. Shops, buildings, road signs, all offer the traveller the consolation that he has arrived somewhere foreign. Ditto Pettigoe after Northern Ireland, with its Victorian shop-fronts, its makeshift-looking customs post made of corrugated iron, and its Bord Fáilte dog snoozing in the middle of the road.

A drink would be nice, we think. Then we remember we are in a foreign country, and we do not have any punts. So we drive back into the tidy North, and go to Irvinestown for a pint in the Central.

I I

The Voice from Tyrone

THE SETTING

The village of Kilskerry lies in Tyrone, just across the county boundary; a river runs through the middle under an old stone bridge. A Union Jack painted on board was tacked up on a telegraph pole. On the village outskirts there were tidy cottages, one with a box hedge surrounding a flagpole on which the Ulster flag fluttered. A few yards further on stood a cluster of beige buildings and battleship-grey Portakabins with a sign which read 'Kilskerry Free Presbyterian Church and Independent Christian School'. The minister of this church (which is that of the Revd Ian Paisley) and the principal of the school is Ivan Foster, and I had come to see him.

There were no murals or climbing frames in the yard. Walking past the classrooms on my way to the entrance, I noticed that the children did not look up from their books, as I certainly would have done under these circumstances – mid morning and a stranger strolling by. Inside the building there was an atmosphere of silent concentration. I could find only one pupil not in class, and she led me to the school office. I knocked, and when the door was opened a moment later, I found myself looking at a man, fortyish, wearing steel-rimmed spectacles. This was Ivan Foster. He did not look like a headmaster, nor did he look like a Loyalist activist.

'Oh,' he exclaimed. He had completely forgotten I was coming. 'I'm with somebody who's come all the way from Germany,' he said, waving at an earnest-looking young man sitting in the office. We put our meeting forward twenty-four hours.

THE INTERVIEW

The next day I presented myself at his bungalow beside the school and was ushered into the living-room. There was a harmonium with a hymnal open on it, a view of the road through a picture window, and a painting drying on the sofa. Bold and highly decorative in a Klimt-like way, it showed an idealized child's house standing in a field of red flowers. It was the work of one of Mr Foster's daughters.

I had come to talk education, and I asked him to begin by summarizing how the school had started. He explained the impetus had originally come from conversations with his wife, then a teacher in the state system, concerning 'indiscipline', and the alarming fact that texts like *Philadelphia, Here I Come!* and *The Catcher in the Rye* as well as authors like John Steinbeck were being taught. 'The language is atrocious in these books,' he said, 'and in this household we do not indulge in that sort of language at all.' He and his wife were also disturbed at the way Evolution Theory was taught in the state system. 'It is taught as a scientific fact, which it is not,' he explained.

The upshot of it all was the private school next door. At the time of our conversation, the fees were about £400 per year, the school was coeducational, and there were forty-seven children attending, ranging in ages from five to seventeen.

'Can anyone send their child?' I asked. Yes, he assured me, all denominations were welcome. Including Roman Catholic? Yes, he said, any parent could send his child, providing he agreed, in writing, that corporal punishment could be administered, and that he would ensure all work assignments were carried out. So, were there any Roman Catholics? No, he said.

We went on to the subject of uniforms, and I asked if the girls' skirts had to be a certain length below the knee.

'Yes, although I don't know if it was ever written down,' he replied. 'You know, we live in this happy little land of Northern Ireland, where things are still very much agreed on by the public with regard to standards, and it hasn't become necessary to write these things down.'

Then he said, I suppose to contradict a feeling that our conversation was dwelling only on the negative, 'I would add that my views on education have expanded greatly since we became involved in Christian education, and I recognize now that there is a very limited curriculum provided in the state schools. God is left out almost entirely. He is left out of it as the Creator and He is left out of it as the orderly governor of all events and all that goes on in the world . . . And leaving all these things out, we feel, has presented children in the state school system with a very unbalanced view of knowledge in its breadth.'

But it was the teaching of Irish history (a minefield, I supposed) which I wanted to know about. 'Do you teach the Penal Laws?' I asked.

'As a Presbyterian,' he replied, a twinkle in his eye, 'I have no hesitation, because the Penal Laws were directed against the Presbyterian people as much as Roman Catholics, and I think we'd be fools not to. Any people of any nation, any race, that is not prepared to learn the lessons of history – not just of the Penal Laws but all history – are fools, absolute fools. Because all they are going to do, if they don't, is keep falling into the same holes their parents fell into.

'Now you asked, "Do we teach the Penal Laws?" Many people have put that question to us, by the way. Yes, we teach the Penal Laws, but I'll tell you what else we teach. We teach the 1641 rebellion as well. We teach the 1798 rebellion, and the slaughter of Protestants that took place during those. *That* is not taught elsewhere. You see – and this is a credit to the propaganda machine of the Roman Catholic Church – embarrassing aspects of Irish history that reflect on the English have been ingrained in the thinking of all within hearing distance of Ireland. However, nobody ever hears about the embarrassing aspects of Irish history that reflect upon the savagery of the Roman Catholic Church.'

I steered the conversation back to the dangers of ignoring history. What did he mean?

'Exactly that. For instance, to take the most obvious example, there is a peace movement —'

'You mean Mr Gorbachov and Mrs Thatcher talking about arms reduction?' I said.

'No, I'm talking on the local level, you know, about here in Northern Ireland.'

'You mean Enniskillen Together?'

'Not them especially but all of the peace movements, and they're saying let's have peace, but they're not asking what the prerequisites for peace are. All they're saying is let's get together now, clap, clap, clap, let's have peace, which is balderdash. The Roman Catholic Church is part of it, and I have to say here that I don't trust the utterances of the Roman Catholic Church ... For instance, go back to the division of Ireland and the setting up of the Free State. The Roman Catholic Church at that time, despite what they said, very much threw their weight in with the IRA ... It's not generally accepted, but they did.'

'But why can't they be trusted?' I interrupted.

'I'll tell you. Despite the assurances of civil and religious liberty contained in the Irish Declaration of Independence, and proclaimed by Church and the rebel organizations, once the Free State came into being, Protestant members of the Southern counties discovered that despite all those assurances, the freedom and liberty which had been promised to them was not going to be. And consequently the Southern Protestant population has largely died.

'My reading of Irish history indicts the Roman Catholic Church as two-faced: they are prepared to back the bloodthirsty rebel in his rebellion when it suits them, and repudiate that same Republican rebel when it suits them.'

'I see,' I said. The Church had practised duplicity during the Troubles (being publicly against but privately for the IRA, promising liberty and then withholding rights when

85

they had achieved power) and they were just as capable of practising duplicity now in the age of reconciliation and ecumenicalism.

'And I feel the IRA, and Gerry Adams and these guys,' he continued, 'they don't get too concerned at the denunciations they face today, because they know that their forefathers faced the same denunciations, but that after a while they became the subject of the song that was sung at the *ceilidh* which the Bishop attended, and he sang and smiled with everybody as they sang the praises of today's hero who was yesterday's subject of the Church's denunciation.'

So were these the lessons of history?

'You have strong views about the Roman Catholics,' I said. 'Do you think that they should exist?'

'Oh, yes, I mean – no,' he said and laughed. 'When you say, "Do I think they should exist?", I certainly wish that Roman Catholicism didn't exist, but those who are Roman Catholics have a perfect right to exist.' He pointed to the window and continued, 'That's a Roman Catholic family over there. And they have a perfect right to resist [*sic*]. And if anyone in this community were to stop them attending the Roman Catholic chapel, they could immediately call on me for assistance to get them to the chapel.'

'Right,' I said.

'I'll get them there. I'll drive them there. And funnily enough, I remember visiting a district preaching, and I gave someone a lift. It was an old lady and when she got in, it was raining, I said, "Where are you going?" Oh, she was going to St Mary's or something you see. And I said, "Grand, where's that? You show me where it is." So on the way there she then sort of noticed that I was a minister wearing a clerical collar. "And where are you going?" she says. "Oh, I'm preaching this morning in the Free Presbyterian Church," I said. And that poor wee woman, I'm sure she had to say three or four masses that day to rid herself of the stain, and the confusion on that poor woman's countenance,' he said and roared with laughter. 'I can still remember it. But the individuals create no problem for me.'

I then asked about integrated schools and he replied, 'I would not have any great quarrel with the matter of integration. It's the philosophy of the individual schools, not the mix of the pupils that bothers me. So let's set aside integration. What I am opposed to in *these* schools is what those who set them up are seeking to achieve through these schools. They are seeking to achieve social and political change through these schools. It's not an educational venture at all, and they make no bones about it. Neither does the minister.* What they want is to change the socio-political thinking of the people of Ulster and to teach them to read and write and that along the way.'

'But the sort of change which they seem to want to bring about, is it so terrible?' I interrupted.

'Yes.'

'To say people shouldn't kill one another?'

'No, no, no,' he said. 'That's not the sort of change they want. They want to accomplish a cessation of the killing. How? By removing one of the combatants and leaving the field open.'

'You mean by removing Protestants?'

'Yes. No, not Protestants, Protestantism.'

CODA

He said he would see me to the car. On the wall by the drive the milkman had left a litre of milk in a plastic bottle. He picked it up and carefully examined the cap.

'I have to be careful,' he explained.

'Why?'

* Dr Brian Mawhinny, under-secretary at the Northern Ireland Office with responsibility for education.

'In case someone tries to poison me.'

I drove away through the brown landscape under a sparkling blue sky. In one or two small fields sheep hid in the hedges from the piercing wind.

Diary

One evening I take my friend from Australia for a walk, one we like, along a small road through rolling countryside. All the houses along the route, originally small stone-built farmhouses and presumably once thatched, have been modernized; asbestos slates, a rendering of pebble dash, PVC windows, fancy stained front doors. There is one exception. It stands on the other side of a brown coiling river spanned by an old stone bridge, a two-storey dwelling like a child's drawing of an idealized house – original sash windows white and shining, Bangor slates glistening with wet, a coat of pink whitewash glowing even in the rain, and a chimney at either gable-end with blue turf smoke curling out of the stacks and disappearing into the grey sky. There are almost no houses like this left, and I have always been curious to know who lives here; this evening as we approach, to our delight, we see that the householders are outside, driving a herd of milking cows across the bridge towards us.

They are a couple in their fifties, a husband and wife I presume. We stop and watch as they drive the wet, nervous animals past us and then through a gate – it is wooden, not galvanized – and into a hilly field of green pasture with a ring of oak trees in a corner.

'Fine-looking animals,' says one of our party.

'Thank you,' says the woman.

She is a foreigner, as we had predicted she would be; she is thin, angular, bony, like Maggie Smith in the The Prime of Miss Jean Brodie, *and as refined an Edinburgh lady under her filthy leather coat as one could hope to meet, right down to her red-painted fingernails.*

'And how many do you milk?' one of us asks knowingly. We have been in the country long enough now to be able to ask the right question,

although not long enough to be able to understand the answer – a figure in litres – which the husband throws at us in a gruff but obviously friendly way.

He is from Northern Ireland, as we had also imagined, and they quickly confirm what we had always supposed. He and she met and married in England, then retired here. The house is his; in the family six generations; he would like to modernize but his 'blow-in' wife will not let him.

We separate into groups. While the others go off to look at the beehives and hens, I go into the barn with the husband. His name (which is too good to be true) is Mr Beak. He is stocky, in his fifties, has faintly mesmeric blue eyes and wears a blue Royal Navy jumper which stinks of sour milk.

Within seconds he is relating his life story: twenty years in the Royal Air Force; then civvy street and a variety of jobs all involving uniforms – security guard, Beefeater at the Tower of London, postman; finally, a nice house in Leicestershire and a small business selling porcelain figurines (again too good to be true) of soldiers. Then, in Fermanagh, a bachelor uncle dies; the farm passes to him; and he retires with his wife to live the good life milking forty cows.

We smoke and stare out of the door of his neat barn, across his immaculate cobbled yard with the geese picking between the stones, over the stack of turf lovingly sheathed with green tarpaulin, and away to the distant bog-coloured hills on which the rain streams down. And as we stare, Mr Beak gives voice to that theme beloved of so many in his position: the awfulness of metropolitan life versus the wonders of the rural.

England, he observes, is completely gone to pot. It is too dangerous to walk around in any more. Nor can you as much as leave your window open without some 'punk' breaking in.

'As for Dublin,' he continues, 'all the housewives on the estates are selling drugs. That's how they make their pin money. It's not safe to go out of your house day or night.'

At our parting he suggests that we might all meet up one afternoon soon and have a pot of tea and a chat.

Returning home, we all agree he has disturbed us, but we cannot explain why this is; after all, he has been perfectly polite and friendly.

12

Politics

A COUNCIL MEETING

It was held in the town hall. On the walls of the council chamber hung the crests of the old district, borough, county and rural district councils into which Fermanagh was divided before the reorganization of local government in the early seventies, as well as the charters on parchment describing the make-up of the crests.

Chairs were arranged in a horseshoe. The Unionist representatives sat on one side, the Nationalist on the other. The Workers' Party councillor and the Non-party councillor were the buffer between them. The atmosphere was thick with smoke.

Motion 8B: that Fermanagh District Council resolves to fly the Union flag of Great Britain and Northern Ireland – the Union Jack – on Enniskillen Town Hall on all bank and public holidays, royal birthdays or other such occasions as directed by the government of the day.

The proposer was Councillor Foster, Unionist. Four years before, the Nationalists (when they'd had the majority) had removed the Union flag from the town hall. With this motion, he said, he was 'putting right a wrong which was imposed on this county and historic town of Enniskillen and the people of Fermanagh by Sinn Féin, supported by the SDLP'.

The flag was British; Northern Ireland was British; ergo, the Union flag must fly.

'We don't need two pages of that sort of shit,' shouted Councillor Cox of Sinn Féin, a fiery, bald-headed patriot.

Councillor Foster, undeterred, continued with his panegyric

to what he called 'the Great Family of Britons' and their inimitable identity with the Union flag.

'It stands for freedom,' shouted one of the Unionists.

'It does not,' shouted back Councillor Cox, his face steaming. The Union Jack represented British oppression, he opined.

Councillor Davy Kettyles spoke next. 'Will this motion shake an angry fist at the Tory government for the way it has effectively kicked in the teeth the pensioners of Britain and Northern Ireland?' he asked rhetorically.

No. Of course the motion had nothing to do with the mighty fight of left and right, which was his concern as the Workers' Party member.

He ended well. 'For me, Northern Ireland chokes on its own symbolism, is poisoned by its own bigotry and is stifled by its own petty-mindedness.' A fair point which no one heard.

Now Councillor Johnston, a DUP member whose formidable quiff gave him the appearance of a forty-something rockabilly, rose to speak. Immediately Councillor Cox began barracking.

'Despite the interjections of gunmen I continue to speak,' thundered back the councillor with the quiff. Then he denounced the unholy alliance of Councillor P. McCaffrey and the SDLP who, when they had taken down the Union flag, 'had been trying to be greener than Sinn Féin'.

The uninitiated could be forgiven for feeling confused at this point.

More interjections from Councillor Cox. 'Not until the flag is down everywhere will Northern Ireland be free from oppression.'

Then the extraordinarily still and heavy bulk of the Unionist, Councillor Coulter, who had sat until that moment without seeming to move or even breathe, suddenly came to life and began shouting, 'Never, never, never.'

Now Councillor O'Kane of the SDLP rose to speak. 'Given

all Councillor Foster's talk of respect for the sovereign and so on, is the implication that he now accepts the rule of Her Majesty's government?' Councillor Foster, whose opposition to the Anglo-Irish Agreement was well known, was seemingly hoist with his own petard, mooted Councillor O'Kane. Not that Councillor Foster either noticed or cared.

Now, at the far end of the chamber rose Councillor Noble, Unionist. He was gentle, wistful and totally inaudible.

At his finish someone from the Nationalist side shouted, 'Cecil's going to buy his wife a pair of Union Jack knickers.'

Hearty laughter echoed round the chamber. I even thought I caught a smirk on the face of the only woman present, Councillor McVitty. Only Councillor Coulter failed to notice the laughter that was resounding as he rose to his feet and began to speak.

Next was Councillor Corrigan, Sinn Féin. He shot to national prominence when, while council chairman, he refused to condemn the IRA bombing of the war memorial in November 1987. He conceded that there was little likelihood of the proposed motion being voted out, as the council currently enjoyed a Unionist majority (which probably had something to do with the bomb, though he didn't mention that), and followed with a not entirely unexpected denunciation of Unionist 'triumphalism'.

Then it was Councillor Lunny's turn, wizened, eighty plus and bearing the scars of many a political battle. He hinted darkly that the secret ambition of Corrigan et al. was to see the Irish tricolour fluttering over the town hall. Then he turned to the Unionists and remarked, 'There [were] some in the room who, if they knew St Patrick spoke Irish, would no doubt want the St Patrick's cross removed from the Union Jack.'

Councillor Ferguson, leader of the Unionists, was next. 'The British government subsidizes every man, woman and child in Fermanagh to the tune of £1,012 per annum, so is it not right and proper to fly the flag?' he asked.

Councillor Corrigan, presumably chastened by Councillor Lunny's masterly innuendo about the secret wish Sinn Féin harboured in its heart to see the Irish tricolour fluttering overhead, now rolled up his metaphorical shirt-sleeves and got stuck into the fray. 'What about collusion between the RUC and the Loyalist murder gangs?' he shouted at Councillor Ferguson.

The motion was carried 12:11.

Diary

This evening, I am told Mr Beak is what is called a well-known character. Without compunction he discharges his slurry into the river. When other householders and fishermen downstream come to his house to discuss this, he hits them; one unfortunate is hit with a brick and his spectacles are broken.

Mr Beak is also in dispute with all his neighbours over water rights and boundaries. An oak is the current subject of contention. It grows on an adjoining farm, but, because roots and branches are partially on his side, Mr Beak cuts down the tree and carts it off. The neighbour comes over to remonstrate and gets his nose broken.

Mr Beak also has it in for the owner of the nearest local shop, for reasons that are obscure. Mr Beak has broken the man's front window, let down the tyres of his van, allowed his cattle to stray into the man's garden, and even shouted at the shopkeeper's young children when they passed in the lanes and made them cry.

With interest I gather that farmers from both sides are united in wishing he would go.

13

In the Market-place

MONEY, THE GREAT LEVELLER

Thursday means market and mart day in Enniskillen. The market stands in front of the old fairground site, where the Irvinestown road meets the South African war memorial. The stall-holders put their stands up on the pavement stretching away from the gates of the mart.

This Thursday as I wandered along, looking at the yard brushes and the pet food, the spanner sets and the imitation Barbour jackets, I could hear the animals on sale bellowing in the mart and the rapid patter of the auctioneer over the PA.

At the corner opposite the war memorial there was a stall selling cassettes. It was manned by a woman with a hard angry stare and a pointed nose.

The cases with their titles showing were laid out flat. At first sight it seemed they were all either Country & Irish – *Philomena Begley Sings Country* – or schmaltz Irish – *Songs of Dear 'oul Donegal*. Then I noticed, to one side, some Loyalist cassettes in what is known as the 'Kick-the-Pope' tradition. There was *Ulster's Glory* for instance, which contained those well-loved favourites 'The Pope's a Darkie' and 'All the Way with the UDA!'

The stall-holder, I decided, was a Loyalist bigot. I was about to turn away, when my eye was caught by a raft of tapes at the other end of the stall. Ah ha, what did we have here? *The Men Behind the Wire and 24 Other Republican Classics, Songs of the Irish Resistance* and *The James Connolly Collection* which, like the Loyalist material, was not short on the odd bit of animus either:

God's curse on you English, you cruel-hearted bastards,
Your deeds they would shame all the devils in Hell,
There are no flowers blooming but the shamrock is growing,
On the grave of James Connolly, the Irish Re-bel.*

If there is one thing that can make a man (or woman) rise above narrow sectarian allegiance, it is profit. This woman, a Northerner (although I could not tell from which community she came), was prepared to sell the worst not only of her own community but of the other side as well. Presumably, because she was making money out of it all, this did not represent a contradiction.

Diary

There is a radio on the shelf above the café counter, and it is announced that David Owen's Social Democratic Party have decided to contest elections in Northern Ireland, the commentator adding that the mainland parties have not been active here for years.

'That's good,' says a man at a table. He is wearing an Arran jersey. As I am behind him, I cannot see his face.

The man sitting opposite him leans forward. He has a pot-belly. He stares at the man in the Arran sweater.

'They're Brits and this is Ireland,' hisses pot-belly. 'We don't want any of them. They can fuck off.'

The man in the jersey rises to his feet. A moment later the bell over the door tinkles as he leaves, and through the lace curtains which hang down behind the windows I glimpse him hurrying away.

Pot-belly sugars his tea and stirs.

---

* 'The Ballad of James Connolly, the Irish Rebel', from *Songs and Ballads of Dublin*.

14

Two Events

FANCY DRESS

The notice in the *Impartial Reporter* said there would be a Hallowe'en bonfire and fireworks display in aid of the rebuilding fund for the local Protestant parish church.

The venue was St Angelo Airfield. I parked on the runway and walked in the freezing cold to one of the hangars. It was crammed with several hundred people eating hot-dogs and puffing on cigarettes. The rector, grey mufti under a car coat, was on a chair speaking into a PA system which whined and crackled. He was trying to organize the fancy-dress competition.

Then, like the Red Sea in the Bible, the crowd parted in two. Tiny tots dressed as goblins and ghouls traipsed between us, anxious expressions on their faces. The winner was a fairy in white tights which wrinkled round her knees. She was given a handwritten placard with which to parade up and down. It read 'Winner in Prettiest Category'.

Next were the seven to nine year olds. One was a burly boy in army fatigues and sunglasses, a burnt-cork moustache blacked on to his face. To his back was pinned a placard which read 'Hands off the UDR!', a reference to the current controversy surrounding the investigation by John Stevens into allegations that UDR personnel had passed sensitive documents to the UVF. Despite the Stevens inquiry those in the hangar clearly had no doubts about the regiment's integrity or the boy's message. When his effort won second prize, he got the evening's warmest round of applause.

The rector, back up on his chair, directed us outside. In the paddock behind the hangar we stood around while the bonfire crackled, then turned our cold faces towards the exploding fireworks. Infants started screaming. They were not used to fireworks, the sale of which has been prohibited since early in the Troubles.

Beside me a mother cradled her bawling child and shouted above the din of the Catherine wheels, 'It's all right, darling, it's not the IRA, it's a firework.'

MY SECOND REMEMBRANCE SUNDAY

I parked near the Ritz Cinema and started to walk. Rain was pouring, thick grey needles of it which froze the hands and face. The streets were deserted except for policemen sheltering in the doorways of shut-up shops, poppies in the headbands of their peaked caps.

Turning into Belmore Street, having seen nobody, I was half-surprised to find the crowd gathered around the war memorial. I went up and found refuge in an entrance to a shop. There were several hundred people, all in their Sunday best.

The band played a cheerful medley of First World War tunes, 'Where's Your Lady Friend?', 'Tipperary' and 'Take Me Back to Dear Old Blighty'.

Banners were then lowered, and, as the rain truly bucketed down, the Earl of Erne (the Queen's representative), Mr Peter Bottomley (a junior minister at the Northern Ireland Office), a representative of the Canadian High Commissioner and members of the police, fire brigade and various British regiments laid their wreaths.

The band played on with 'Nearer My God to Thee' and 'Lead Kindly Light', while townspeople filed out to lay their wreaths. Several were men and women who had lost relatives in the bombing two years before. Mr Robert Houston, the brother of Mrs Bertha Armstrong who died in the blast with

her husband, Wesley, told the *Irish Times*, 'I am disappointed
... I thought that something would change as a result. Sadly
I have to say it hasn't.' *

The only local politicians who attended the ceremony were
from the OUP. No SDLP or Sinn Féin councillors took part,
and the DUP council members refused to attend in protest
against the Anglo-Irish Agreement and the presence of Mr
Peter Bottomley.†

Diary

During a walk in the day I come across this piece of graffiti:

> *Ulster says 'No'*
> *But Del Monte says 'Yes'*

*Our friend T —, with whom we have supper, explains the second line
is incomplete and should have continued:*

> *... and he's an Orangeman.*‡

* 13 November 1989.
† ibid.
‡ The Del Monte orange juice television campaign, to which the graffiti
refers, featured 'Mr Del Monte' squeezing suitably ripe oranges and nodding
sagely, while happy orange-pickers in the background shouted, 'He say,
"Yes."'

15

The Bomb – 1987

SATURDAY NIGHT

The St Michael's Reading Rooms, into the ruins of which I had so ghoulishly peered on my first walk around Enniskillen, was originally a school. However, at the time of what has come to be called the 'Poppy Day Massacre' it was an active Catholic social club, owned by the Church but run by its own committee. It was a place where Catholic men met to play snooker and where pensioners gathered for bingo.

At seven forty-five on Saturday, 7 November 1987, Jim Dunlop, the caretaker of the building, opened up for bingo; the session continued until ten twenty.

After the players had left, Jim Dunlop and a friend, Eamon Goodwin, stayed in the building and played poker with Seamus McCarney, a youth of fourteen and the son of Seamus McCarney, the committee secretary, and his friend Damien McGurn, aged sixteen. Mr Dunlop described what happened next in a report quoted in *The Times*:

At about eleven forty-five p.m. Damien thought he heard footsteps upstairs. He said, 'There's a movement or something. There's somebody up there.' Sean said he thought he heard it as well. We told them, 'It's the old building,' as we often heard it crack [*sic*], but they kept saying they could hear something.

We couldn't hear anything but they kept insisting so after about fifteen minutes, for the sake of them being scared, Eamon went to the foot of the stairs and threw open the door and shouted 'Who-ever's out there had better not be,' but there wasn't anybody.*

A NOTE

The next day was Remembrance Sunday, known informally as Poppy Day. In the British Isles it is the Sunday closest to 11 November, the anniversary of the armistice of 1918 that ended the First World War. After 1945 the occasion was expanded to include the dead of the Second World War, and the process of inclusion has continued. Today Remembrance Sunday commemorates those who died in all the twentieth-century wars, and among the dead there are many Irish nationals from the South, as well as many from Northern Ireland.

That great numbers of Southerners died is surprising to some, because of Ireland's neutrality in the Second World War. In fact Ireland has a long military tradition, with a good deal of service being to the British Army. Many Irishmen fought and died in the First World War, and when the first ever Remembrance Sunday ceremony was held in November 1919 the island of Ireland was part of the United Kingdom.

In the Free State after Partition the ceremony slipped from the official calendar. As one historian of Irish War memorials has described it, there was 'abuse and shameful neglect'† of the war memorial park designed by Lutyens at Islandbridge (now properly restored at long last). Services on Remembrance Sunday continued, as did the sale of poppies, but these activities were discreet. At best they were tolerated and at worst they were regarded with positive hostility because they were British and a sign of the ancient connection with Britain.‡

* *The Times*, 10 November 1987.
† Jane Leonard, 'War Memorials' in *Ireland and the First World War*, p. 64.
‡ One can get the feel of this from the correspondence columns of the Irish newspapers, for instance in the early 1980s when the Irish Army became

The motivation behind this is the need, always acutely felt in Ireland, to create a separate identity from that of Britain. In Ireland the shedding of the cultural apparatus of the occupier, that familiar post-colonial phenomenon, has been impossible in the military area (as in so many others as well). Despite seventy years of separate administration, the Republic and Britain are still inextricably bound up with one another. Men from Southern Ireland have continued to serve in the

---

involved in the Remembrance Sunday ceremony in Dublin organized by the Southern Irish branch of the British Legion. This, for example, is what one correspondent wrote to the *Irish Times*:

> When the First World War started, Redmond and the Irish [Parliamentary] Party were the unquestioned leaders of the Irish people. Politically corrupted by association with the House of Commons and craving for personal acceptance by the British Establishment, Redmond advised the youth of Ireland to join the British Army to fight for King and Country. It was a dreadful error of judgement.
>
> It took the blood of Patrick Pearse and the men of 1916 to correct it. But in the meantime 250,000 of our young men answered Redmond's call to British arms, and 50,000 of them left their bones in the French Flanders, Gallipoli and Mesopotamia.
>
> It would be an ill-informed and ungenerous Irishman who would regard these men as any less patriotic than those who stayed at home to fight the Black and Tans on the streets of Dublin and Cork, and in the flying columns throughout the country.
>
> But recognizing the patriotism of those who joined the British Army in the First World War is a very different thing from accepting the British Legion for what it is – a British organization operating in Ireland (20 October 1983).

In a letter the following day, Peggy Lemass O'Brien, sister of Seán Lemass (Fianna Fáil taoiseach, 1959–65), directly connected the animosity to Remembrance Sunday (and specifically the participation of Irish soldiers) with the current Troubles:

> At the time of his retirement from politics he [Seán Lemass] said, 'The Irish people should never forget that it was more humane to be murdered in the gas chambers than to be dragged to death by a Black and Tan tender or to die of starvation in a land of plenty or to be butchered by Cromwell.'

British Army – about 42,000 in the last war.* And it goes on. As Robert Fisk notes at the end of *In Time of War: Ireland, Ulster and the Price of Neutrality 1939–1945*, his colossal study of Anglo-Irish relations,

When the final British casualty lists were published [at the conclusion of the Falklands conflict], there was something familiar about them. One of the first British seamen to die in the South Atlantic came from Northern Ireland. And among the last to be killed fighting for the Crown was a young man from the Irish Republic.†

In Northern Ireland attitudes to Remembrance Sunday were very much the reverse of those in the South. Participation was official state practice. Ulstermen – especially proletarian and Protestant ones from Belfast and its hinterland – joined in considerable numbers after 1914, and overall the community backed the war, having recognized that the demonstration of commitment would not go unremarked elsewhere in the Union. Ulster's finest hour, militarily speaking, came on 1–2 July 1916; in the attack on the German lines at Thiepval 5,500 officers and men were killed, wounded or subsequently declared missing in action. Many of these would have formerly been members of the Ulster Volunteer Force, and in 1914 had been ready to fight the British in order to remain British. The

---

As 'descendants of an old Timer' my family and I are horrified that Irish soldiers should attend a British Army Remembrance service while the veterans of Derry's Bloody Sunday are still torturing Irish men, women and children in the Six Counties and British spies are openly working to destabilize the Republic.

The inference here, that the organizers of Remembrance Sunday, the British Legion, were Fifth Columnists, was openly declared by Lieutenant-General Michael Costello, a retired officer of the Irish Army, who accused the Legion of being 'a source of information on events in the country for British Intelligence' (*Irish Independent*, 23 September 1984).

* Robert Fisk, *In Time of War: Ireland, Ulster and the Price of Neutrality 1939–1945*, p. 524.

† ibid., p. 576.

loyalty of the Unionists had doubtless seemed irritating and inconsistent in peacetime, but on the battlefield they showed themselves to be pure gold.

The Second World War saw Ulster – or, to be precise, Protestant Ulster – reaffirming its commitment to the Crown. There was a Home Guard known as the Ulster Defence Volunteers, and by 1941 in the regular British Army there were 23,000 recruits from Northern Ireland, all volunteers.* (Conscription had been avoided, though Unionist politicians hungered for it.)

On 15 April 1941, 180 Luftwaffe planes unloaded more than a hundred tons of bombs over Belfast's residential areas; 745 were killed in one night. On 4 May 204 Luftwaffe planes returned; they dropped 95,000 incendiary devices on the shipyard's harbour area, killing 150, damaging 56,000 houses and levelling 3,200. The intention was to devastate the war production machine, which it did. Yet Northern Ireland recovered. She was loyal and, as she always boasted, hardworking. By the end of the war the Province had built 140 warships, 10 per cent of the entire merchant marine of the UK, 1,500 heavy bombers, and innumerable guns, tanks and shells.† It was an extraordinary achievement, for which the reward was the extention of the welfare state to cover Northern Ireland. The Unionist majority were not keen; they sensed it would lead to trouble. Attlee, however, got his way, and Northern Ireland emerged from the Second World War just as she had from the First: closer to Britain than when she had started. British state ceremonies continued to occupy a central position – perhaps were treated more seriously than in the rest of Britain, because Northern Ireland felt threatened – and of these, Remembrance Sunday was one of the most important.

* Robert Fisk, *In Time of War*, p. 522. By 1945 the total number from Northern Ireland who had served in the British Army was about 38,000. This was less than the number from the South, but then the population of Northern Ireland was smaller.
† R.F. Foster, *Modern Ireland 1600–1972*, pp. 558, 561.

SUNDAY MORNING

In Whitehall, in front of the Cenotaph, at about a quarter to eleven on the morning of Sunday, 8 November, the massed bands of the Guards were playing the fixed repertoire of music used on every Remembrance Sunday; they had just begun Sir Edward Elgar's 'Nimrod' from the Enigma Variations, a piece which is always included in the programme as a tribute to the innocent victims of war.

Security was tighter at Whitehall than it had ever been before, because it was feared that the IRA were anxious to stage a big attack to compensate for the setbacks of the previous year. Veterans entering Whitehall had to pass through metal-detector gates before they were allowed to take their places. The medals many wore naturally slowed the process down. Hundreds of uniformed police were on duty among the thousands of spectators who lined Whitehall as far as Trafalgar Square.

At Buckingham Palace the Queen and the Duke of Edinburgh left by car for Whitehall.

Meanwhile, in Enniskillen, in the lumber room of St Michael's Reading Rooms, a bomb which had been left there, weighing between thirty and fifty pounds, exploded without warning.

The explosion blew out the gable-end of St Michael's Reading Rooms under which more than sixty people were standing. Those below were hit by a solid wall which then broke up. They were simultaneously caught by the traffic barriers along the front of the pavement. These, which had been put there for their safety, decreased their chances of survival. Police, troops and firemen who had been standing by, waiting to take part in the Remembrance Day parade, broke ranks to dig with their hands.

In London the quiet of the two minutes' silence was interrupted only by a child crying and by the faintly audible messages being relayed on police radios, as marksmen kept watch from the roof-tops above.

Throughout Britain the same silence was observed at thousands of similar ceremonies.

At Heathrow Airport all flights were held back for five minutes, so that aeroplanes would not disrupt the services along the flight paths. In the airport terminals, as at war memorials and in churches and chapels, passengers stood silent.

A single salvo from the First World War cannon on Horse Guards Parade sounded the end of silence in Westminster, and buglers of the Royal Marines began 'The Last Post'. Around the foot of the Whitehall Cenotaph a carpet of poppies began to grow as wreaths were laid. Royal British Legion members, bowler-hatted and carrying rolled umbrellas, began their march past. There was special applause for limbless victims in their wheelchairs and the blind party, white sticks swinging in unison. The bands began their medley, beginning with 'It's a Long Way to Tipperary'.

In Enniskillen the first of the dead were being taken off to the temporary mortuary in the Territorial Army Centre. Ambulances were ferrying the injured to the Erne Hospital. James Mullan, who had been attending the ceremony, drove his terrified son Adam home. It was then he remembered his own parents. They had been standing in the crowd near St Michael's. He returned, searched the rubble and learned they were both dead.

Billy Mullan and his wife Agnes, known as Nessie, died together in the explosion. Adam, their grandson, could have been with them, as they usually stood together. But this Sunday, Adam had become separated from his grandparents and had felt too shy to cross over the road to them.*

Another victim was Georgina Quinton; she had been waiting by the war memorial, wearing her Second World War medals. The others included Kit Johnston, a former ambulance driver, and his wife, Jessie, a nurse at the same hospital;

* *The Times*, 10 November 1987.

Johnnie Megaw, caretaker in the Imperial shopping arcade; Ted Armstrong, an off-duty policeman; Wesley Armstrong, a British Telecom engineer and former customs officer, and his wife, Bertha.

From the war memorial crowds were now making their way up the main street to St Macartin's Cathedral (where the northern aisle is set aside as the Inniskilling Regimental Chapel, and where on Remembrance Sunday a service is traditionally held). There were angry shouts directed across the road at the crowd standing in front of the Catholic church: 'Have you seen what *you've* done? Have you seen what *your* lot have done down there?' As a way of souring relations between Protestant and Catholic, it was an inspiration to attack a Protestant ceremony from Catholic property, for it reinforced a long-held Protestant suspicion that between the Church and the armed struggle there is a symbiotic relationship.

All over the islands journalists telephoned politicians and public figures for their opinions. Mrs Thatcher described the bombing as an act 'desecrating the dead and a blot to mankind'. The Revd Ian Paisley, leader of the DUP, broke his Sunday silence to denounce the massacre as a 'diabolical deed by hell-inspired monsters'.

But it was John Hume, leader of the mainly Catholic and Nationalist SDLP, who made the most pertinent comment. He said it was 'probably the most deeply provocative act to have been committed against the Unionist people'.

That was exactly what it was. One, the ceremony which had been targeted allowed them to demonstrate their Britishness (although many Roman Catholics participated). Two, Enniskillen was a town which had a long tradition of military service to the British Army. A rise in tension between the two communities was to be expected, but it did not happen. This was because one man turned the other cheek, with the effect that, whatever anger they felt privately, Protestants found it impossible either to express it or to act on it.

The man was Gordon Wilson, a Methodist and father of the youngest victim, Marie, a girl of twenty and a trainee nurse. On Sunday night he gave his first interview:

We were only there about fifteen seconds when the bomb went off. It wasn't a loud explosion. I was pushed forward on my face and the rubble of the wall and the railings fell on top of us and I thought I was not badly hurt.

I then felt somebody holding my hand. It was Marie and she said, 'Are you all right, Daddy?' I said, 'Yes.'

I asked her if she was all right, and she said, 'Yes.' She was crying all the time, so I asked her about four or five times. When I asked her the fifth time if she was all right, she said, 'Oh, Daddy, I love you very much.' I knew then there was something wrong. Those were her last words.

Marie Wilson was taken to hospital; she received twenty-six pints of blood, but ten minutes after coming out of surgery she died. She had suffered brain damage, a crushed pelvis and severe internal bleeding.

My wife Joan and I do not bear any grudges. We don't feel any ill-will to those who were responsible for this. We see it as God's plan, although we do not understand it.

I shall pray for those who did it. May God forgive them.*

The same evening the chief constable of the Royal Ulster Constabulary, Sir John Hermon, was giving a press conference. He disclosed that another bomb had been planted at another Remembrance parade at Tullyhommon, near Pettigoe, thirty miles north-west of Enniskillen, on the border. This bomb was a 150-pound landmine with a command wire which stretched into the Republic. The bomb was never activated because a farmer unknowingly broke the wire when he was out on his tractor early on Sunday morning. He also revealed that Enniskillen was very nearly an even greater disaster than it had been: 245 children would have been

* Gordon Wilson's interview with the BBC is quoted extensively in *The Times*, 9 November 1987.

standing outside the St Michael's Reading Rooms at the time the bomb exploded, but for the fact that the band they were marching behind was running three minutes behind schedule.*

MONDAY

Edwin Graham, Pauric Dolan and other local people decided to arrange a vigil and had posters advertising the event printed up.

Gordon Wilson gave his second interview to the BBC:

I bear no ill-will. That sort of talk is not going to bring [Marie] back to life. She was a great wee lassie. She loved her profession. She was a pet and she's dead.

She's in heaven and we'll meet again. Don't ask me, please, for a purpose. I don't have a purpose. I don't have an answer, but I know there has to be a plan. If I did not think that, I would commit suicide. It is a part of a greater plan and God is good and we shall meet again.†

Eleven people died; sixty-three were seriously injured; and one victim, Ronnie Hill, is still in a coma at this moment of writing.

TUESDAY

The headline of *The Times* on Tuesday, 10 November 1987, was 'Defiant IRA puts blame on the Army'. The Provisional IRA statement of the previous day was published:

The IRA admits responsibility for planting the bomb in Enniskillen

* *The Times*, 10 November 1987.
† ibid.

yesterday which exploded with such catastrophic consequences. We deeply regret what occurred.

GHQ has now established that one of our units placed a remote-control bomb in St Michael's, aimed at catching Crown forces personnel on patrol in connection with the Remembrance Day service but not during it. The bomb blew up without being triggered by our radio signal.

There has been an ongoing battle for supremacy between the IRA and the British Army electronic engineers over the use of remote-control bombs.

In the past some of our landmines have been triggered by the British Army scanning high frequencies, and other devices have been jammed and neutralized.

On each occasion we overcame the problem and recently believed that we were in advance of British countermeasures.

In the present climate nothing we can say in explanation will be given the attention which the truth deserves, nor will compensate the feelings of the injured or bereaved.

In the same issue Gerry Adams, president of the Provisional Sinn Féin and MP for West Belfast, extended sympathy on behalf of 'the Republican people' to the families and friends of those killed. He said, 'I do not try to justify yesterday's bombing. I regret very much that it happened.'*

Marie Wilson was the first of the victims to be buried.

The organizers of the planned vigil went into Enniskillen with their posters only to find what they had not expected: that every shop was shut. Shock and the long round of funerals had closed the town down. Anticipating a small turn-out, they decided to make just 200 mimeographed sheets of hymns for everyone to sing.

In the town hall a special meeting was convened by Paul Corrigan, Sinn Féin leader and council chairman, at which he expressed sympathy to the bereaved. The ten Unionist members of the council boycotted the meeting. After asking those present to join him in silence 'as a mark of respect to those

* *The Times*, 10 November 1987.

who have lost their lives', and standing with his head bowed, he offered Sinn Féin's 'sincerest sympathies' to the bereaved and injured.

Asked by *The Times* correspondent if he did not consider the time inappropriate to make such comments, Paul Corrigan said, 'I don't think so. I believe what happened on Sunday is part of an ongoing struggle over the last eighteen years, and however appalling and tragic it might have been, it has to be looked at in the overall context of that struggle.' When then asked to condemn the bombing, he replied, 'I won't condemn bombings in general. I support the right of the IRA to wage military actions against the occupation forces. I won't condemn the acts of a movement that attempts to overthrow and wrench from Britain the right to self-determination.'*

WEDNESDAY

The Times headline of Wednesday, 11 November, read 'Thatcher steps up pressure on extradition'.

In Enniskillen there were funerals all day long.

In the evening rain poured and 2,000 people squeezed into the Diamond in the town centre for the vigil. There was no organized service and no organized church presence. The hymns were sung; every one reassembled at the war memorial; and then they went home.

THURSDAY

The Times headline on Thursday, 12 November, was 'BA cleared to bid for ailing B-Cal'. The bomb might have slipped from the front pages, but in Enniskillen the vigil had created a

* *The Times*, 11 November 1987.

sense of expectation. All those I have spoken to have agreed, there was an odd feeling in the town afterwards. So perhaps there was something in the newspaper slogan 'The spirit of Enniskillen'. People wanted a direction into which to channel what they felt.

ENNISKILLEN TOGETHER

This was the organization which sprang up eventually to channel all those feelings. Their aim was to promote activities where Protestant and Catholic could work together, and from the start they have concentrated on three key areas: the arts, the churches and education.

After establishing themselves, Enniskillen Together approached the council for a seeding grant. They were awarded £200. Four Sinn Féin councillors asked to be recorded as dissenting from the decision, and one, Brian McCaffrey, said he did not agree 'to giving money to organizations which don't tackle the real problems'.*

Enniskillen Together are not the first group to have attracted flak in Northern Ireland, but the group which have probably earned the most opprobrium must be the Peace People, who similarly arose as a spontaneous reaction to violence.

In the summer of 1976 a car driven by members of the IRA, who were being pursued by members of the security services, ploughed into the three children of Anne Maguire, killing them all. After the funeral the children's aunt, Mairead Corrigan, spoke publicly. She emphasized that she held neither party to blame but added the killing had to stop. Joined by

---

* *Fermanagh Herald*, 11 June 1988. Enniskillen Together also attracted criticism from the Unionist side. Bert Johnston of the DUP described the Ulster Project (a scheme to send teenagers of both religions to the USA, which Enniskillen Together were involved in organizing) as 'sick'. See *Fermanagh Herald*, 15 July 1989.

Betty Williams and Ciaran McKeown, the Community of the Peace People (to use their proper title) was formed.

In its first phase the movement held large rallies in Belfast and other centres in Northern Ireland. In addition there were rallies by supporters in Dublin, London and other points abroad. Then in 1977 the organization switched their efforts to arranging meetings of small groups, especially in areas of confrontation. They also began encouraging community efforts, the provision of better recreational facilities and even in some cases the establishment of local industry. The leaders of the Peace People also started criticizing established politicians. In 1980 there was serious internal dissension within the movement, although not apparently on policy. Peter McLachlan, the chairman, Betty Williams and Ciaran McKeown all bowed out. This left, of the original founders, only Mairead Corrigan, who was chairwoman until 1981 (when she married Jackie Maguire, husband of her sister Anne, who had committed suicide the previous year. She was said to have been heartbroken both at the loss of her children and at the continuing violence). In 1986 Mairead Corrigan claimed the split in the movement had arisen because their German backers would provide money only on condition the Peace People avoided controversy, and that they were not prepared to do this.

Today the Peace People are still going. Although extremely media shy, and with popular support less than it was in their heyday, they are still receiving backing from several countries, including Norway. Among their current activities are regular camps for young people in Scandinavia, a five-a-side football league in Belfast designed to bring Protestants and Catholics together, mixed group holidays in Britain and Europe, helping the families of paramilitary prisoners, and running prison buses for relatives.*

These are the dry facts, but what I remember of the Peace

* W.D. Flackes and Sydney Elliott, *Northern Ireland: A Political Directory 1968–1988*, p. 220.

People in the second half of the seventies is a different story. First, they arrived in a blaze of glory, and for a moment it looked as if they really might pull some sort of *rapprochement* between the communities out of the bag and oblige the paramilitaries to give up. The next stage was that they came in for a lot of criticism from the politicians; the Nationalists were especially virulent about them. But the ire of the politicians was only to be expected, given the way the Peace People had seemed, almost recklessly, to rub so many of them up the wrong way, and in a sense the condemnation they received from the *status quo* only enhanced their street credibility; if the hardmen were rattled enough to denounce them, then the Peace People had to be on to something.

And the organization would have weathered these storms, I believe, had it not been for the next stage – which was the counter-reaction. When they first arrived, popular opinion (and the press) had seen the Peace People as Northern Ireland's salvation and had largely created them in this image. However, it wasn't long before it was realized that they, no more than anyone else, could not deliver peace with a capital 'P'. The failure to match impossible expectations wasn't really the Peace People's fault, but what was perceived as *their* failure left a bad taste in the mouth of the expectant; the pendulum swung away from them, and this was then picked up by the press.

Next in the story, inevitably, after such a meteoric rise, was the fall – the *coup de grâce* being a 'fur coat' which it was alleged one or both of the Peace People's women had bought from the Nobel Peace Prize money the organization had received. On the strength of the insubstantial allegations the media had a field day; and, having created the Peace People as heroes, they now indulged in that most popular of journalistic occupations (and, incidentally, a great seller of newspapers): knocking down the once great and trampling them in the mud. Northern Ireland was poor then (it still is), and these claims touched a raw nerve among both communities; to this day, the 'fur coat' remains a symbol of duplicity.

Whatever one thinks about them, the Peace People are an object lesson for any group wishing to harmonize community relations and end the violence in Northern Ireland. Thus, Enniskillen Together, with their example to learn from, have been extraordinarily cautious from the start. They have opted for practical measures rather than making large promises (peace with a capital P). They have set about satisfying what they have identified as some of the community's needs, rather than doing it the other way round and trying to impose on the community institutions which will 'improve' them. Such moves are always rejected; they smack of social engineering. The road to harmony, it is their understanding, is not achieved with a bang but with a long, slow slog.

Diary

'What did the bomb mean to you?' I ask my host, after we sit down to eat.

'I was at home here,' he says, 'and I got a call from my mother and she said, "— has been killed." He was a dear family friend. My mother was very upset. I decided to go over and see her. I couldn't get into Enniskillen; the centre was completely closed off, of course. So I had to go round the side of town through the estates. Do you know the Kilmacormicks One and Two?'

I nod.

'Well, then, you'll understand. In those estates there were groups of young people on the streets, and it was as if their football team had won. I suppose I shouldn't be surprised. There were years of gerrymandering and everything else behind it.

'Up to that point I'd always thought of the IRA as somehow the Robin Hoods. All the terrible wrongs and the things which the politicians talked about, but which they didn't do anything about, they were setting them right. But after the bomb I decided they were just Al Capones.

You know, you got so much to kill a soldier. So much to drive a booby-trapped car. So much to plant this bomb in Enniskillen.

'The writing's on the wall, only we Prods haven't seen it. Leaving the violence aside, there are more Catholics being born in this Province than Protestants, and eventually they'll outnumber us.

'We have to make our peace, but I see very little evidence of this on the Protestant side. We have the likes of Mr Paisley, who lives in an area which is 80 or 90 per cent Protestant, talking in the way he does. It's all very well for him to go on like that, he doesn't actually have to meet with Catholics, but down here in Fermanagh, we Prods, we simply haven't had that numerical advantage.

'Our period of grace is running out. We have ten years — twenty at most. And if we don't make our peace in that time, then when a United Ireland comes, as inevitably it will, we'll be fucked.'

16

The Missing Chapter

In one draft of this book the chapter which appeared next was entitled 'Reconciliation'. It was based on an interview with a Roman Catholic nun who had made friends with members of the security services and their relatives who had been injured by the bomb at the Enniskillen war memorial, and with other members of the security services and their families whom she met as a result of these contacts.

However, prior to publication and following an approach from the subject and a letter from her solicitor, it was agreed to withdraw the chapter, although it was innocuous. All offers to alter the chapter in order to meet her objections were met with a blank refusal to discuss the matter in any way whatsoever. Clearly the watchwords of the besieged in Derry, 'No Surrender', have passed into wider use than one would expect.

Diary

It is a cold and wintery day. I arrive at the appointed spot on the Belfast road ten minutes before proceedings are due to start. Cars are lined along the hard shoulder.

I park and get out. Men, mainly middle aged, mainly rural, many of them in their farm workclothes, are silently gathering. There are 600, perhaps 1,000.

They place themselves in a line along the edge of the road where they can see the traffic and, more importantly, where they can be seen by passing cars. And then they stand there, a rebuke to every passing motorist. *They are demonstrating their opposition to the Anglo-Irish Agreement and their support for the UDR.*

I wander up and down the line. A few are talking about crops and Christmas. I do not hear the Anglo-Irish Agreement mentioned once.

After an hour of crushing boredom and cold, there is a sudden dash for the cars, because the sixty minutes of protest are up.

Making my way to my car, I notice an abandoned placard reading 'Ulster says "No"'. It is wet and curling at the edges.

PART THREE

WINTER

17

Troubles

I

Troubles, the word, is used to describe two events: the Anglo-Irish War of 1919–21 and the conflict in Northern Ireland from 1969 to the present day. The Troubles I am talking about in this chapter are the former.

The period is popularly believed to have been a time when the whole of the island of Ireland was engulfed in an all-out, no-holds-barred death struggle between John Bull and the IRA.

In fact there were wide regional variations in the levels of violence. In Munster, the south-west and the border area of Ulster, the army and the IRA fought bitterly. Meanwhile the west of Ireland was militarily quiescent, while in Co. Fermanagh there was so little strife that the author of a Nationalist local history, Peadar Livingstone, is happy to assert, 'The IRA were not very active in Fermanagh during the War of Independence.'* Unionists agreed. In the opinion of Sir Charles Falls, the county council solicitor, in January 1921, 'Fermanagh is the most peaceful, law-abiding county in Ireland.'†

Why? Livingstone suggests the IRA realized that 'activity . . . might lead to fierce civil strife on the part of Catholic and Protestant'. One can see what he means from this passage:

The Fermanagh Brigade [of the IRA] planned to demolish the vacant Lisbellaw [police] station in early June 1920. The local

* Peadar Livingstone, *The Fermanagh Story*, p. 286.
† ibid., p. 293.

Unionists had advance notice of the raid, and they were prepared. These men were members of the Ulster Volunteer Force, which still lived on in Lisbellaw, and they were soon to become the nucleus of the B-Specials. They scattered about the town and waited the arrival of the IRA. About one thirty a.m. two men with bicycles entered the village. They walked up and down the street and decided that the coast was clear. They rattled on the school gates as a signal to their companions that the situation was all right. In a few minutes some IRA men, from the Enniskillen direction, entered the village. They broke up into two groups and started to bore. Meanwhile the Unionists lay about in the darkness, watching the Republicans. Suddenly a shot broke the silence. The Unionists rang the church bells to summon help. Thereupon the firing became general . . .*

With the army and the RIC to deal with, the IRA obviously had no wish to take on the Unionist population as well. But their considerations in this matter were not simply logistical. Storming Fermanagh (or other areas with large numbers of Protestants) was also to be avoided, because it would have muddied their case: which was that the enemy against whom they were struggling was the Anglo-Saxon occupier rather than their compatriots who happened to be Protestants or Unionists. This animus did not emerge until after 1921.

II

The Anglo-Irish Troubles of 1919–21 were ended by the Treaty. Dáil Éireann finished debating this agreement on 7 January 1922. The discussion was fractious, but what is surprising is what the points of friction were.

The Treaty gave away a great deal more than Home Rule – agreed and then put on hold at the start of the First World

* Peadar Livingstone, *The Fermanagh Story*, p. 287.

War – had ever offered. It provided complete independence in domestic affairs, including full fiscal autonomy, and external freedoms, given the way dominion status was currently changing, were also implicitly wide. It could not be faulted on these fronts.

Nor was Ulster – which was to remain British – the stumbling block; for the Irish delegates who negotiated the Treaty and many in the British government believed that the projected Boundary Commission (which Clause 12 of the Treaty would create) would restore Fermanagh and Tyrone to the South at the very least, which in turn would deprive Northern Ireland of a third of her land area and call her viability into question. There was considerable vagueness about exactly how the commission would work, whether its mechanisms would involve plebiscites, and, if so, on what basis they would be established, but faith there was on both sides that it would succeed.

The Treaty also granted Britain the right to the continued use of three important naval bases on the Atlantic coastline of Ireland, and this – hard as it is to imagine today when military rights have become such a major source of friction in post-colonial situations – was not the major source of contention either.

Where the animus centred was on the matter of the Oath of Fidelity (as it was coyly termed, the word 'Allegiance' having been jettisoned as provocative). This recognized the Crown. Whatever the pragmatic arguments for accepting the Treaty (and as the pragmatists in the Dáil debate pointed out *ad nauseam*, it contained, as the Home Rule bill had never done, the potential for complete independence), in the eyes of the irreconcilables and the visionaries in the Dáil, accepting the Oath would have, as one contemporary historian has neatly put it, 'made the bloodshed of the previous two years meaningless. [They] . . . repudiated the Treaty arrangement, not because it failed to deliver a United Ireland, but because it failed to deliver the "Republic",' that imaginary place wholly untainted by any association whatsoever with the British Crown.*

The Irish delegates who had negotiated the Treaty with Lloyd George and signed it can hardly have been surprised by the argument which raged. But signed they had, and the matter had to go to the vote.† It was very close: 64 in favour, 57 against. And the split in the Dáil was mirrored in the country, although it would be a mistake to imagine it was as even. Among the population those pro the Treaty probably had the edge.

III

A period of confusion then followed in the new Free State, as the forces for and against the Treaty aligned themselves in readiness for the impending civil war. However, along the border with the new Northern Ireland state the two sides sank their differences and resolved to protect Catholic areas against the incursions of the 'security forces' of the new Belfast government, i.e., the Ulster Special Constabulary. This force was comprised of A-Specials (full-timers), B-Specials (part-timers and the largest part of the force) and C-Specials (reservists).

The original kernels for the Special Police were vigilante forces which had been organized in six or seven places in Northern Ireland during the Troubles. Among the most successful of these was that founded by Sir Basil Brooke in the summer of 1920. This group was centred on the demesne at Colebrooke and armed with old Italian guns which had been run into Larne for the UVF before the war.‡ Those men at Lisbellaw who ambushed the IRA detachment who

---

* R.F. Foster, *Modern Ireland 1600–1972*, pp. 506–7.
† Among them was Sean O'Mahony, the representative from Fermanagh.
‡ Brian Barton, *Brookeborough: The Making of a Prime Minister*, p. 31.

had come to blow up the police barracks had the same pedigree.

Recruitment of the Ulster Special Constabulary started in November 1920. It will come as no surprise that only Protestants joined. By January 1922, when the Treaty was ratified, they were not only an established force, but one which had already acquired for themselves a reputation for animosity towards Nationalists and Catholics. Here is Livingstone's catalogue of their behaviour:

A member of the Specials walked through the streets of Tempo with a loaded rifle and threatened to blow a Catholic lady, who happened to be standing on the street, to blazes. James McHugh was coming from Ballyconnell when A-Specials seized him and took him to a sandpit. They forced him to go down on his knees and ordered him to curse the Pope and the King [sic] and say 'God Bless the Specials' . . . A-Specials halted children at Derrylin and questioned them about their religion . . .

The paragraph continues:

Many Catholics got notices ordering them to quit Fermanagh. The following letter was received by James Magee of Killee, Ballinamallard. It was headed 'Ulster Defence Association' and dated 6 June 1922:

Take notice that you must clear out of Ulster within four days and remove your belongings and save a fire. We must have the house clear on Sunday at latest. If you disregard this notice, you will get Waterloo. Signed, Descendant of William III, since the Battle of the Boyne.

Bawnboy Rural District Council and the provisional government in the Free State launched a scheme to assist refugees from Northern Ireland, who were pouring into the larger towns.*

In the way Livingstone organizes his material, there is a clear connection between the Specials, illicit Loyalist activity and the enforced emigration of Catholics.

Yet on the 'other side of the house' a completely different

* Peadar Livingstone, *The Fermanagh Story*, pp. 305 ʿ

truth about the Specials obtains. In Unionist folk memory to this day the Special Constabulary, the B-Specials especially, continue to be revered as stout defenders of the infant Northern Ireland state against its enemies within and without, and the view is taken that they were rather more sinned against than sinning. This is Livingstone again, and his catalogue of some of the difficulties the Special Constabulary had to contend with in the early twenties is the sort of evidence supporters of the force would invoke:

There were many incidents on the night of 7 February 1922. IRA cut down thirteen telephone poles at Clontivrin. They seized a house, belonging to Richard Ward of Kinturk, and held it. Specials tried to dislodge them and a battle raged for two hours before the IRA retired. A Crossley tender of Specials was ambushed at Wattlebridge. IRA men kidnapped twenty members of the Specials in the Newtownbutler area. S-Constable George Phair was wounded in the arm in an ambush and taken to Ballybay. From here he was brought to Carrickmacross to be exhibited in a cage in the fair . . . Meanwhile twenty Protestants from County Monaghan sought refuge in Newtownbutler.*

The problem of competing truths is certainly not new. Thackeray highlighted it over a hundred years before these events in the conclusion of *The Irish Sketch-Book*: 'To have an "opinion about Ireland" one must begin by getting the truth; and where is it to be had in the country? Or rather there are two truths: the Catholic truth and the Protestant truth. The parties do not see things with the same eyes.'† Trying to determine absolutely where right lies in the matter of the

---

* Peadar Livingstone, *The Fermanagh Story*, p. 305. The cage reference is an exaggeration. What happened, it appears, was that Phair and others, after their capture, were being taken by lorry to prison when their IRA captors decided to exhibit them at Carrickmacross, where there was a market in progress. A hostile crowd gathered around the lorry but were dispersed by the IRA guard who fired over their heads. See the *Fermanagh Herald*, 23 February 1922.

† William Makepeace Thackeray, *The Irish Sketch-Book 1843*, p. 401.

Special Constabulary is exhausting and ultimately fruitless. It is also a mistake to leave the IRA out of the account. In their development the two were intimately connected, and their effects on each other were largely negative.

Trying to determine right is also to miss the point of what was occurring in the twenties. Society was dichotomizing into Nationalist and Unionist camps. These had vastly different and antagonistic aspirations, and the IRA and the Specials were their champions. With views so far apart it was inevitable that structures would follow suit, and that conflict would follow. And when it did, it took the form of systematic violence and intimidation associated with land ownership and territorial sovereignty based on clan or blood lines – what is elsewhere known as a vendetta.

IV

It began early in 1922, shortly after the debate in the Dáil, when IRA forces started to attack across the border, killing several Special Constables, who in their turn killed several IRA men. The IRA began their attacks in the Rosslea area in the very south of the county, and then worked their way northwards, attacking Belcoo and Garrison. Finally, in the early summer, they occupied the flat northern part of the county and the villages of Pettigoe and Belleek at either end of it. The government had to send two regiments armed with howitzers, and they only succeeded in evicting the occupiers after a fierce battle. The incident came up in Parliament during a debate on the 'Irish Situation', and Winston Churchill – then the colonial secretary and the minister who had sanctioned the operations along the border – commented, 'The Sinn Féin party has got to realize, once and for all, that they will never win Ulster except by her own free will, and that the more they kick against the pricks, the worse it will be for them.'*

* *Impartial Reporter*, 29 June 1922.

V

Sixty-seven years later Winston Churchill might have had cause to repeat himself as the old pattern reasserted itself.

Early in the evening of Monday, 27 November 1989, a man on a tractor was lured to a house at Corry, Belleek, where a man and wife were being held hostage. A number of masked and armed men seized his Massey Ferguson, and 500 pounds of explosives were packed into the link box.

About nine o'clock the RUC barracks in Belleek came under fire from the Cliff Road area across the River Erne on the Co. Donegal side, and the policemen inside found themselves trapped. An RPG-7 rocket was launched, but it missed the barracks and struck the gable-end of a disused house. Police returned fire, and during the exchange the tractor was driven by its owner to the front of the station (the other side from where the firing was going on). The tractor was followed by an Opal Kadet taken from the couple at Corry. Its passengers were the armed and masked men who had packed the tractor with explosives, and they were presumably making certain the tractor driver did as he had been told.

These men now returned to Corry, released the couple and then vanished. Simultaneously, alerted both by the firing and by telephone calls from the police, residents in the area of the barracks began to evacuate the area, helped by the local fire brigade who, as it happened, were drilling at the time in their station just across from the barracks.

Twenty minutes later the bomb went off. No one was killed, but the area in the vicinity of the bomb was wrecked. The West Fermanagh Brigade of the IRA later claimed responsibility.*

These events were not anything like on the level with the outright occupation of the summer of 1922, yet they were part of that tradition, and it is worth remembering that for a few

* *Impartial Reporter*, 30 November 1989.

hours the police had been locked in their barracks, and the IRA had been free to do what they wanted.

I would have to go up to Belleek, I decided, and have a look.

Diary

We are in Co. Cavan in the Republic, heading north. Two old men direct us towards Derrylin. We turn on to a narrow road described as an 'Unapproved Border Crossing' and head on.

Further up there is a signpost. Travellers expecting an indication of the approach of Northern Ireland would be disappointed, for all that this one says is

Fermanagh County Boundary

The explanation for this is that the South does not recognize the border established by Partition in 1920, so the only boundaries which are acknowledged are the old county ones, rather than those of 1920. This is peculiar when you consider that the county boundaries are as 'impure' or Anglo-Saxon in origin as the border, for they were part of the British administrative structure imposed on Ireland, along with the courts, the English language and driving on the left.

So what makes them more proper or respectable than the border agreed in 1920?

18

The Fall of Ceauşescu

I

I drove north towards Kesh, along the same road by which the British Army regiments had moved towards Pettigoe and Belleek sixty-eight years earlier, dragging their howitzers behind. On the radio it was reported that President Ceauşescu was addressing a crowd in Bucharest. Although there had been riots and protests during the previous week, especially in Timisoara, trouble was not expected, said the news reporter. The Securitate would make certain of that.

II

I came into Belleek from the east, the same direction as the soldiers, rather than by the other road from the south, which would have brought me past the factory where Belleek china is made. I stopped at the top of the village main street. It was broad and lined with shops, and at the bottom it kinked round to the left and disappeared from sight. I knew from my map that what lay beyond was the bridge which spanned the Erne, and on the other side of that was the Republic. It was easy to see why Belleek had been occupied. It literally straddles the border.

It was the week before Christmas. In the shop windows I glimpsed shimmery decorations, messages written in artificial snow and a Father Christmas or two. But then, slowly cruising down the street, the Xmas ephemera gave way to shop-fronts boarded with plywood. It was nearly a month since the bomb, but plate-glass windows were not yet replaced. Presumably the Northern Ireland Office had not yet stumped up.

At the bottom of the main street I turned, not left towards Co. Donegal, but right, up a small lane towards the RUC barracks. The signs of damage were worsening. Houses without doors and windows; houses without tiles and their roof timbers showing like ribs; houses leaning sideways, looking as if they had been hit by a hurricane.

On the right loomed the fire station. The front was missing – blown right off, I presumed. Lengths of steel hawser dangled from its stressed concrete walls and floors. Next door stood the health centre, a mess of breeze-blocks, cable, splintered wood, tiling, piping. There were dumper trucks carrying the debris away, and men from the Northern Ireland Office and the insurance companies, neat in their suits and ties, striding about with clipboards and biros as they assessed the damage.

Fifty yards further on stood the barracks, the object of the bomb, a Mad Max pile of steel and concrete fortifications with impressive telecommunications equipment to call for reinforcements, if any should be needed. Inside the pillbox beside the gate a nervous young soldier peered out at passers-by, only his eyes and gun visible to the world.

I got out and looked for signs of damage, but the barracks was seemingly unscathed. Two years before, blast shields and new fortifications had been added in anticipation of just such an attack. The casualties, therefore, of this bomb – luckily there had not been any human ones – had been the houses in the vicinity, the health centre and the fire station. The attack had punished the village.

III

I parked the car and started wandering around Belleek and talking to anyone who would talk about the bomb. The story which began to emerge from the multiplicity of conversations, though not factually different from the one in the newspapers, had a quite new emphasis. Everyone, without exception, commented on how lucky it had been that no one had been killed, and from the questions I then asked the following picture of the night emerged.

After the IRA launched their rocket, there was a hiatus, with people keeping their heads down and staying indoors. Then, since there was neither shooting nor an explosion, they emerged from pubs and houses and started making their way home.* The Bridge Club was meeting in the Carlton Hotel. The members who had come up from the South to play got into their cars and immediately left.

Meanwhile, at the barracks, minds were presumably very much concentrated on the fact that a tractor had been parked at the front. But while the soldiers and police could see this vehicle, everyone else in the village – because of the curious position of the barracks behind and away from the main street – could not, and they were blithely unaware of it as they rushed about.

Some twenty or so minutes after the bomb had been parked, a telephone call was made by someone in the barracks to the local parish priest with details of the 'suspect device'. It was as the parish priest was making his way into the village to warn people that the Semtex bomb in the tractor went off.

With villagers still making their way home or otherwise moving about, and with Belleek not exactly being a large place, by rights somebody should have been caught by the blast. It was only a complete fluke that nobody was killed, and this was the point which was made by everybody to whom I talked, as often as not in the same words, 'It was a miracle no one was hurt.' It was.

---

* From past experience everyone in Northern Ireland knows that after an incident it is important to get home; if you don't, the security services arrive, the area can get sealed off, and you can find yourself unable to leave for hours.

IV

In a pub a customer told me the sad story of his parents-in-law. They had had a bungalow across the road from the barracks which they had built themselves, over a number of years, and at considerable expense. But now – bang! – it was destroyed. It was going to need rebuilding from scratch.

'They've lost everything,' he said in a melancholy way, and *then* he said, 'It was a miracle no one was killed.'

He then went on to talk about the compensation his in-laws were in line for, if and when it came, and as the conversation switched to this area, with others in the pub joining in, I gathered the general view of the bombing among the villagers was that it was an inconvenience, even a grotesque inconvenience, but that if someone had died that would have given the affair a whole different complexion. But nobody had, so clearing up afterwards was simply a practical matter, rather than one informed by grief or emotion.

In another pub, an empty one, I quizzed the barmaid. She lived over the border, not far from Ballyshannon, Co. Donegal (where the West Fermanagh Brigade of the IRA, who claimed responsibility for the bomb, are supposedly based), but worked in the North. We talked about what a Nationalist was.

'You can be a Welsh one or a Scottish one, and you're not assumed to be a supporter of violence,' she said, 'so why can't you be an Irish one?'

'Are you?' I asked.

'Yes.'

'But not a violent one?' I pressed.

She ignored the question – presumably because the answer was self-evident – and started explaining the local situation, as she saw it. 'What's the barracks doing in Belleek?' she demanded rhetorically. It was indefensible, sited where it was. The IRA could just sit across the river and snipe at it till the cows came home; but for the Garda on the other side defending it, it would have gone a long time ago.

And if the barracks wasn't in Belleek, she continued, then the bombing wouldn't have happened. It was only because of the barracks that the IRA came in. They wanted to shift the British. 'If the British weren't in Belleek in the first place, then the IRA wouldn't need to come in, would they?'

'A United Ireland, is that what you're suggesting?' I asked.

'No, for now, just put the barracks further inland,' she said, 'that way it wouldn't be so easy to get at.'

Reading between the lines, I selected, I thought, a practical expression of the classic soft Nationalist approach. No need to sweep the barracks away, just resite it, the unstated implication being that then, in time, when the 'situation' allowed, it would go altogether. In other words Justice today and a United Ireland some time in the future.

I could follow the logic, yet it left me feeling uncomfortable. The argument, which underpinned the proposal, that the bombing was the consequence of the siting of the barracks seemed like saying that the responsibility for the bombing lay with the barracks alone, which left out the bombers, like the argument that rape is the fault of women who 'ask for it' by wearing 'provocative clothing' leaves out the rapist and his decision to inflict violence. The old discussion point from ethics lessons at school returned to me. Someone throws a stone at a man standing in front of a window, but at the last moment he moves and the stone breaks the window. Whose fault is it: the man who moves or the thrower of the stone?

V

In a third pub I got the same argument, this time from the landlady, that the siting was to blame. 'No barracks, no Brits, no Brits, no bomb,' she said.

'Okay,' I answered, 'but there wasn't any need to plant the bomb, was there? The IRA did it and caused the damage which we can see, but they didn't have to. What are we talking about? Pavlov's dogs? See barracks, must plant bomb.'

She laughed, and then I mentioned how damaged the pub had looked on the outside.

'Are you going to get compensation,' I asked, 'and is the damage as bad as it looks?'

Worse, she told me. The pub had lost its roof; the windows had been blown out; and they were still waiting for the Northern Ireland Office to assess them. And *then* she said it, 'It's a miracle no one was hurt.'

'We pay our taxes, you know, we're entitled to compensation. It's the law,' she continued and turned on the radio. Abba thumped from the speakers, and our conversation turned to the price of Christmas turkeys.

VI

I came out of the pub after three. The sun was low on the horizon. In the car I turned the radio on. After his speech in Bucharest Ceauşescu had been whisked away by helicopter from the roof of the Central Committee building, and he had fled. At the time of the bulletin the dictator was still at large, but his capture by army units was expected imminently. In the time I had been in Belleek, the Romanian *ancien régime* had fallen.

A dumper truck, piled high with bomb debris, rattled by, and a man in a suit tapped on my window with his biro.

He was a loss adjuster. 'Do you happen to know where I can find —'s Bar?' he wondered.

'Over there, that's their pub,' I said, 'and I'm sure they'll be very happy to see you.'

Diary

'We never talk to people about the Troubles, unless they're outsiders,' says the wife of the couple I am having dinner with. We have spent the evening talking about nothing else.

This is something outsiders must take on board. The Troubles here are not the dominant subject of conversation; but when a stranger appears, the inhabitants rightly assume that is what they want to talk about, and so they oblige. This gives the outsider the impression that the community are continually talking about the matter, which they are not.

This has been highlighted for me over the last few days, because Christmas has caused me to abandon research; I do not talk to anyone about the Troubles, even once, and nobody mentions them to me either. My attention is entirely on ordinary domestic matters, and the violence is almost invisible, except for the helicopters from the UDR base which roar over our roof morning and evening, as they head for the border with their bellies full of soldiers.

News does filter through from the media, but my reactions are parochial. If the one o'clock news reports a policeman killed in Northern Ireland, I listen. But if the man has been killed in Armagh or Down, my attention drops. If Fermanagh, my concentration rises; if Enniskillen, it is acute.

While all this is true, there is also a contrary truth, which I can feel nagging at me even now as I write. I am seemingly untroubled by the conflict, yet there is an ancient, reptilian part of my intelligence which is continuously reminding me of it — by asking where I am, what newspaper the stranger I am talking to is reading, whether the collection box on the bar is for the Franciscan Church Ross Nuala Building Fund or the Royal National Lifeboat Institution.

This reptilian intelligence is also the supervisor of conversations of labyrinthine complexity, the purpose of which is to uncover the religion and political orientation of whomever I am talking to without, if possible, giving anything away about myself. So while the Troubles might not appear in conversation, at an unconscious level they are a continuous preoccupation.

On the night of the dinner mentioned above, while driving home, I see a car some way ahead down the dark road start to reverse towards me. The reptile warns there is a checkpoint hidden round the next corner. He also does a quick check of my recent alcohol consumption. Then I go round the corner; and sure enough, there they are: fifteen policemen in flak jackets with machine-guns – and all from a glimpse of a tail light.

19
Hard Green

I

It was a wintery dusk, with the light fading fast. I drove along a yellow concrete farm lane. There are such lanes all over Northern Ireland, because, for a while, the government gave farmers grants to build them.

The house at the lane's end was dark. Perhaps no one was in? Then I noticed a dark figure in the entrance of one of the sheds opposite. It was Paul Corrigan, Sinn Féin councillor and sometime chairman of the Fermanagh District Council.

Everyone who saw the television news bulletins at the time of the bombing at the war memorial would know his face; he was the man in the suit with the harassed look who would not condemn the bombing.

I got out and introduced myself, and it was odd for the next few moments, as it always is with someone whose face is familiar from television. They look just like the person you remember from the small screen, and yet they are not that person; they are a bad copy of the television version.

We went into a kitchen-cum-living-room. It was cold. The stove appeared to be out. He sat on the sofa, stretched his legs out, and waited for me to begin. I took the armchair. There was no small talk. He had cut his finger and it was bleeding, but when I suggested tending to it, he brushed the idea aside. I could see this was going to be the kind of interview where I would ask my questions, he would answer them and that was all that would happen.

II

'In your time as a councillor,' I asked, 'what's given you the most pleasure?'

'I think in 1985,' he said, 'when the council fell to Nationalist control. I had great pleasure in that sense of well-being which Nationalist people felt at the time. Despite discrimination, gerrymandering, we'd proved that none the less we could win . . .

'However, that sense of euphoria was ill founded. The council didn't have the power and the control that Nationalist people thought it had. They associated the council with all sorts of things which the council weren't able to do any more. With road building, for instance. The DOE who do the road works are still called council workers. No more.' Then he continued, 'Oh, I remember how difficult it was to get roads tarred in Catholic areas in my young days, whereas in the Unionist areas the roads were tarred years before. That was just one example of the discrimination we put up with.'

'And what was your worst moment on the council?' I asked.

'Losing four seats. We lost four seats in the last election, and we lost control of the council. It was very disappointing. I could see that three would go, but there was one we were very sad to lose. We lost it by a hair's breadth. We shouldn't have lost Erne East. We lost it to Jean McVitty. There was a split Nationalist vote. The transfers didn't work. She won without reaching her quota.'

'Are you saying she didn't get enough votes or that she got more votes than each of the two Nationalists?'

'She got more votes than each of the two Nationalists,' he admitted.

'Did the bomb at the war memorial affect the last election?' I wondered.

'I wouldn't say so. It wasn't mentioned on the doorsteps to me when I was canvassing. I didn't meet a single person who said, "I'm not going to vote for you because of the bomb." I think the Unionists agreed. I saw Ferguson in some interview

I read saying that he didn't think it was an issue. I don't think it was big at all, at all.'

III

The conversation turned to the subject of Eastern Europe. We agreed the two Germanies would unite. Too much momentum had already gathered to prevent it. I said that though the two Germanies and their desire to unite were often invoked as an example in Ireland, the two situations really couldn't be compared. 'For a start,' I said, 'here people are killing one another.'

'I'd like to take you up there,' he said quickly. 'The division in enmity here was fostered and created by the British. They created the problem of enmity for the purpose of trying to conquer the Irish people. They fostered division among the Protestant and Catholic people of the country. It was so much easier to partition the country, you see, once the divisions were sewn. It's been the *modus operandi* of the British all over the world: divide and conquer. Yet I believe if the British withdrew, or made guarantees of their intention to withdraw at a future date, the vast majority of Unionists would accept the situation and would be happy to live in a United Ireland. But because the British won't withdraw, and because of being privileged citizens – which is only human nature – the Unionists don't want to relinquish power. By remaining in Ireland, the British encourage them. I know many Protestant people who have said to me they would be quite happy to accept a United Ireland for the sake of peace and tranquillity.'

IV

'In Sinn Féin's discussion document 'Scenario for Peace'* the principal precondition of British withdrawal is the disarming

---

* Which describes itself as an 'answer to those who claim there is an alternative to the continuation of British rule'.

of the UDR and the RUC. How do they feel about that, do you think?'

'You'll have to ask them. I know some Protestants will leave. In that document we say provision will have to be made by the British government to repatriate certain people.'

'I notice the document, while it says the RUC and the UDR will have to be disarmed and disbanded before Britain withdraws, makes no mention of the IRA or the UVF.'

'If Britain declares it no longer has an interest in remaining in Ireland and states that it intends to withdraw, there will no longer be a necessity for the IRA.'

'The IRA will vanish?'

'I would certainly think so. I would hope so.'

Diary

I slip into a country bar for a quiet half hour and sit down at a table by the fire. There is a man on the stool at the end of the counter, and he turns round to look at me. He is heavily built and has a round, cherubic face. It is difficult to guess his age: he could be mid twenties, or he could be late thirties. He sees that I have my notebook open, and that I am writing in it.

'I've always wanted to write a book,' he says.

He stops, and, as he stares into the distance, his fingers wriggle like the legs of a dying insect.

'You write this down now,' he says brusquely. 'I was a young lad, right. Eight, nine, ten, you know, knew nothing. Not about politics anyhow. And I was out in the street with the other lads, and we were kicking a football up and down. And then a man came pedalling down the street, and he was a B-man, a B-Special.'

He took a drink and continued. 'He had on his uniform, and a shiny gun was slung over his shoulder, and he was going off to shooting practice. Although his name was Woodley, my grandparents called him "sir", and my people called him "sir", but do you know what he was to me?'

'*No.*'

'*Just plain Charles Woodley, never "sir" or "Mr".*'

'*I see.*'

'*The parents were brought up to say, "Yes, sir, no sir, three bags full, sir," but we're educated. Maybe that's why we've all these Troubles we have now. We just won't say "sir" any more. We just fucking well won't say it. Now you write that down and you sign it, A. Fenian.*'

20

Hard Orange

Immediately after Paul Corrigan I had arranged to see Bert Johnston, one of the two DUP councillors. In a small place, where details of movements are soon known, I wanted it to be clear that the spirit of even-handedness informed my research.

Bert Johnston lived in Ballinamallard, the village which was supposedly the Loyalist of the Loyal, which I had passed through on my first visit to the area, and which had puzzled me because it had no flags or other symbols. His neat, modern house stands in the centre of the village beside his upholstery business.

He brought me into his thickly carpeted living-room. The plate on the wall read 'Giving thanks always for all things unto God'. There was an electric organ in the corner with a cassette on the top titled 'Blessed Assurance' and a pair of tiny red Dutch clogs holding a biro. There was also a lot of upholstery around: heavy printed cotton curtains with wide pelmets, matching table-cloths, and a heavy taupe-coloured material covering the three-piece suite.

We sat opposite one another. There was tea out of fine cups and scones off fine plates. He was a slim, neat man, and in his appearance he was as studied as his furnishings. On his feet he wore black velvet slippers with a feline motif on the side, set off by white socks.

'Can you sum up your party's beliefs in a nutshell?'

'The DUP believe the Northern Ireland people are best served in the United Kingdom,' he began. 'They're on the right wing of Unionism, but they believe in the National Health Service, a free education system, and so on.'

'Why are you in the party?'

'Because they provide good strong leadership, because of the charisma of the leader, and because I believe the policies are right for the Province. The members of the party, like myself, are mainly fundamental Protestants.'

'Meaning?'

'The members are mainly people who believe in the Reformation principles.'

'Which are?'

'The Reformation principles emphasize the supremacy of the Bible, as Martin Luther came to realize. There is opposition to the Mass as well. I come from that sort of background. It's not so much an English thing as something Scottish. I myself come from Scottish stock.'

'What denomination are you?'

'I'm an Independent Methodist.'

'What's that?'

'I hold to the old tradition of Methodism as enshrined by John Wesley. I'm an Independent Methodist rather than a Methodist because of my opposition to ecumenicalism. Most Methodists favour dialogue with Rome. The Methodists in the Irish Council of Churches certainly do.'

II

'So what do you feel about Roman Catholics as opposed to Roman Catholicism?'

'I'm very pleased you asked that question. Roman Catholics, excluding members of Sinn Féin, I'd like to show them that I love them and that the Lord Jesus died for them. As for the Church, I hate it, for it misleads them. They trust it, and it's going to fail them. They have a personal faith in Lord Jesus Christ, but that is only a simple faith in Christ's finished or completed work on the cross. They pray for the dead, which is completely unscriptural, because the Bible makes clear, unless you accept Christ, you'll be lost in eternity for ever. Remember, the Bible says no praying could get a rich man out of hell when he was in it.'

. After outlining the doctrinal differences between the various Christian traditions, we moved on to capital punishment, during the discussion of which he got up without pausing for breath and returned, saying, 'I've got the Book here. It answers all the questions,' then read out the scriptural authority for capital punishment which he had just quoted, Genesis 9:6, '"Whoso sheddeth man's blood, by man shall his blood be shed: for in the image of God made he man."' He had got it right, word for word. He smiled and closed the book.

III

'Do you accept the claims made by those who struggled in the civil rights movement, that Catholics were discriminated against?'

'I can't see how they were discriminated against. Many had jobs and still have to this day. Some of the things they fought against – the business vote – I don't think were all that unfair. Now what we have is someone with no property and someone who owns property, both having the same vote. In some Commonwealth countries, if you have a business, you get another vote still.

'But then when they got one man one vote, what many Unionists found so nauseating was they then looked for PR. People began to ask where it would ever end. And now people are asked their religion when they become employed. Where will it end? I don't think I have the right to ask somebody who comes to work for me what his religion is. At the day's end his religion isn't going to give me any better work out of him. We're always looked on as being backward in this part of the world, as obsessed with religion and what everybody is, but we're not, and yet now we have a government and British ministers forcing us into trying to find out, and setting up the Fair Employment Agency.'*

'The FEA say that a Catholic is two and a half times more likely to be unemployed than a Protestant.'

'Roman Catholics generally tend to have bigger families. The reason they're unemployed is because they get more money than by working. Some Roman Catholics have admitted this to me. And some Protestants must similarly ask themselves, "Why work when I can get more on benefit if I don't work?" I've worked on jobs, and Catholics have left to go on benefit, saying, "It's better." I don't blame them. It's the way the Social Security is geared that's wrong; it pays a person more to be unemployed. It may be morally wrong, but practically it's right what they are doing.'

'Catholics and Nationalists say they don't get work because they're persecuted and oppressed and have suffered because of this.'

'I don't believe they have suffered in the past. After all, their numbers have increased, and they have the same rights when it comes to claiming benefits or anything else the state provides.'

IV

'What do you think of the Anglo-Irish Agreement?'

'It's undemocratic. The Unionist people had no say and no input into it. Yet the SDLP did. Even if it was something Unionists would like, it's still morally wrong, because they had no input into it.'

'So what's going to happen?'

'I haven't any crystal ball. I think there'll be an end to the Anglo-Irish Agreement. It can't survive – it hasn't

* The Fair Employment Agency, now recast as the Fair Employment Commission and having greater powers.

majority support. Besides, it hasn't done what it was supposed to do.'

'Do you foresee a devolved parliament?'

'That's difficult, because Unionists won't enter a discussion about parliament until the Agreement is scrapped.'

'What do you call yourself, what do you regard as your nationality?'

'My nationality – I'd be British. But then Scotsmen are British. It's my passport which tells me what I am. My passport tells me I'm a member of the United Kingdom of Great Britain and Northern Ireland – that's what it tells me I am, so that's what I must be.'

*

The conversation was over. We turned to the subject of antiques, and he showed me two beautiful comb-backed chairs, and a rosewood hoop-backed chair which he had restored. After admiring them for some minutes, I pulled on my coat and said, 'Thank you very much,' and he said how very nice it had been talking to an intelligent Catholic.

Diary

On the radio at lunch-time Thomas Boyd, leader of the Glasgow Rangers Supporters Club (Belfast branch), is interviewed.

Disgusted that Rangers have signed Mo Johnston, a Catholic, the branch have dissolved themselves.

'Isn't this the behaviour of old-fashioned bigots?' wonders the interviewer.

'Well,' the interviewee responds, 'if that's the term people want to apply, then so be it.'

I am left wondering if the word 'bigot' has now acquired a previously unknown value, and has become the appellation of the pure, of those who resist dilution.

21

Belfast

PETER

We met in a small room on the Falls Road, West Belfast. There was a fire in the grate, and he bent as close to it as he could.

'Burn everything English except her coal,' he said and laughed. 'That's what they say around here.'

He entwined his spindly legs and stared at me. The skin on his face was like parchment, and when he coughed his whole body trembled. Emphysema.

Peter was from Ballymurphy Estate. Built as part of the post-war slum clearance programme, it was intended to be mixed. Because it was far from the centre, it had few shops and no services. Everyone who could got out, and in effect it was the Protestants who went; this left the Catholic inner-city transplants behind. Ballymurphy is one of several similar estates which today comprise West Belfast.

'It was desperate in the beginning,' he said. 'For the first few years the children in Ballymurphy couldn't do the full day in school. There wasn't room because the Church didn't provide enough of a school to give them a whole day; so half came in the morning and half in the afternoon. That was how much the Church thought about us.

'Incidentally there was no church either, and when we got the church finally, no parochial house for the priest. That's how much they liked us. He'd just come in each Sunday, say Mass and go out again.'

A residents' association was established, and £6,000 collected to build a community centre. They needed more but doubted help would come from the council who, the Bally-murphy people believed, perceived them as dirty, unwashed, lazy, alcoholic, Catholic nonentities. The association hired a public relations company whose other accounts included Gallagher's Tobacco and Harland & Wolff, the shipbuilders.

They said, 'You've got £6,000, haven't you, in the bank? Okay, buy £6,000 of city bonds and we'll get your picture in the paper with the caption "Ballymurphy backs Belfast but does Belfast back Ballymurphy?" They did and that was the beginning.

'Next step, we got this statistician from Queen's; he was English, as a matter of fact. With his help we did a survey. We discovered, for instance, that we had 450 houses, and that in fourteen years 12,000 families had passed through. Ours was a transit area for people going on to better things, only we were the ones left behind.

'We got all this information together, and we were all ready to publish, and then internment came and I was lifted. The man from Queen's came to see me in prison. He said to me, "Peter, I don't think this is a very good time to publish." So we held off, anyway until I was out. That would have been '74. Then we published. We got tremendous flak, but it was worth it, just to get the truth down in black and white.'

A DRIVE

I made the obligatory drive – first over to the Shankill, where my guide showed me some graffiti which read, 'No Pope Yet', to which some wit had added 'Fucking Lucky Pope', and then back to the Falls. We drove past terraces of redbrick houses; sprawling new estates; stretches of waste ground filled with pieces of glinting glass; empty streets where boys played football with burned-out cars for goal posts; liquor shops with grilles over the windows; walls and gable-ends with graffiti, childish, amorous and political, scrawled on them; and everywhere we went we seemed to run into the 'Peace Line'. It is not, as the term suggests, something like the Berlin Wall, a big, ugly, brutal divider, so much as a series of devices – observation posts and culs-de-sac, high walls between streets and entries made impassable by obstacles – which at first sight appear to be part of a town-planning programme, but on closer examination are obviously part of a system designed to make the movement of people between areas difficult if not impossible, and the movement of the security services swift and easy. Peace Line is the wrong name but presumably deliberately chosen because anything more accurate, like 'Conflict Inhibitor' or 'Social Controller', would not do.

On the car radio, appropriately, there was a programme from the Berlin Wall. I listened to an interview with a schoolgirl on a trip, who explained that she had just hired a hammer for a dollar and chipped away a piece of the Wall for herself. 'Ah, capitalism,' sighed the interviewer. A schoolboy in the same party thought Checkpoint Charlie had been bought by an American millionaire and was being airlifted to Nebraska.

DEIRDRE

We entered South Belfast, leafy and prosperous, while on the radio the description of the schoolchildren and their journey continued; souvenir bits of Wall safely stowed in their pockets, they had left Berlin and were heading south for Munich.

My destination was the Peace House, the headquarters of the Peace People, a large and prosperous-looking building, originally a manse. Deirdre, whom I had come to see, was one of the staff. She was a well-dressed middle-aged woman. As soon as we sat down, I related the view I had heard expressed in West Belfast earlier, that IRA violence equalled self-defence.

'Self-defence!' she exploded. 'It just isn't true, is it? The

IRA aren't fighting the army when they come and want to search their houses, or stop them in the street and question them. They're defending themselves by sneaking up and shooting them in the back, or sneaking up to policemen's cars and putting bombs underneath them. That doesn't sound like self-defence to my way of seeing things. That just sounds like pure cold-blooded murder.'

The telephone rang. It was a journalist, and he asked what she thought of the irony: the Berlin Wall was not only down but was being demolished by souvenir hunters; meanwhile the Peace Line not only remained but somewhere at that moment was being extended.

'You see, the big difference between the Berlin Wall and our wall,' she said, 'is this. That was a wall designed to stop people getting together; ours is a wall designed to keep people apart. Neither side in Berlin wanted the Wall; here we both want the wall, because we're frightened of what the other side will do to us, and even of what we may do to them.'

Diary

He tells me this story. When he is in his late teens, Mairead Corrigan of the Peace People comes to visit Enniskillen. A branch of the movement starts in the town, and he becomes the secretary. His parents, whom he describes as 'Unionist but not Loyalist', are not entirely happy with this.

At the New University of Ulster [Coleraine] he remains involved. One Wednesday in February 1978 he is travelling up to Belfast to the Peace House, when he hears on the car radio that at Maghera, Co. Londonderry, a UDR man bringing his children to school has been killed by a booby-trap bomb under his car, along with his daughter, while his son has been badly injured.*

---

* They were William John Gordon, a 39-year-old corporal in the regiment, his ten-year-old daughter Lesley, and his son Richard, aged eight.

He arrives at the Peace House to find that Betty Williams, Mairead Corrigan and Ciaran McKeown have decided to picket the Sinn Féin office in the Falls Road because of the killings.

Twelve of them go down, including the narrator. The Falls is quiet: just a few pedestrians who stare at them curiously. Suddenly the area empties and goes silent. Then, in all the little streets around them, they hear the women banging dustbin lids – the traditional call to arms when soldiers approach the community.

A crowd assembles on the other side of the road and begins shouting abuse. The picketers have made their point, and Ciaran McKeown decides it is time to move on. They move down the Falls and into Grosvenor Road with the mob following, several hundred strong by this stage, and led by a group of women who start shouting at Mairead Corrigan, 'Where's the fur coat? Where's the Nobel Prize money?' and so on. Mairead Corrigan replies to her accusers. The 'banter' that ensues slows her down; the picketers get separated from each other and suddenly the narrator finds that he and Mairead Corrigan are a long way behind the rest of the party.

Feelings are rising. The women begin to pull Mairead Corrigan's hair and jostle her. He steps behind her to prevent the pushing and pulling. At last the mob have the target they have been waiting for. Young men surge forward, knock him to the ground and begin to kick him.

'The funny thing,' he says, sounding utterly serene as he describes the experience, 'is that when you're in that sort of a situation, with all your adrenalin pumping, you see things with extraordinary clarity.

'When I am on the ground, I notice a gateway into a small park a few yards away. Realizing it is my best chance, I crawl into it like an animal, and that restricts how many can kick me at any one time.'

At this point the women move forward and pull the youths off. The narrator believes this is because, as he's put up absolutely no resistance, they see there is no point in continuing. They're not going to get anything out of him.

The mob move off, and his colleagues from the Peace People return. The narrator gets up and begins to walk away with Mairead Corrigan.

22

Peacework, Policework

THE MORNING SESSION

It was a conference on the future of the Royal Ulster Constabulary organized by the Committee on the Administration of Justice.* The front page of the programme showed a photograph of two laughing RUC men on Comic Relief day, red clown noses jammed on and weapons at the ready. It was like a Diane Arbus picture, and I wondered, as I arrived at the venue in Belfast, if I was in for a police-bashing exercise, full of knee-jerk platitudes about brutality, unnecessary force, etc.

The keynote speaker was a grey-haired man from Haringey Borough Council, and he delivered, in a nasal twang, a speech which was like an editorial from the *New Statesman* in the eighties. The United Kingdom was slipping towards totalitarianism, he said, and the deterioration was most advanced in Northern Ireland.

I had come in through the Falls, and, on the basis of what I had seen through my car windscreen, the man from Haringey had a point. I had seen an arrest. Protected by a ring of soldiers with boot polish on their faces and guns at the ready, RUC men, guns cocked, had bounced a shouting suspect into the back of an armoured Land Rover. The odds were twenty-five to one. This was not ordinary policing. The suspect was

---

* The Committee on the Administration of Justice is an independent civil liberties organization formed in 1981 to work for 'the highest standards in the administration of justice in Northern Ireland by examining the operation of the current system and promoting the discussion of alternatives'. From *Lay Visitors to Police Stations in Northern Ireland*, CAJ Pamphlet No. 14, p. 1.

terrified, but so also, judging by their expressions, were the soldiers and the police.

JOYRIDERS

Over lunch I sat with Mary, a social worker and a native of West Belfast, with black curly hair and the palest blue eyes, and Veronica, an English woman with healthy red cheeks and blonde eyebrows, a member of a religious order who worked with a reconciliation group on the Peace Line.

As we ate hard, greasy chops, Mary told me that 80 per cent of the considerable number of cars stolen in Northern Ireland each year were dumped in West Belfast, and it was probable that 80 per cent of the Province's joyriders were from the area.

'So that's where the police would recover my car,' I said, 'if it should ever be stolen.'

'Only they wouldn't get it for you.'

She smiled. (Mischief, apology, embarrassment – I could not tell.)

'It might have been burned out because of fingerprints. Alternatively it could have been booby-trapped. You'd have to get it yourself, but that would be too dangerous. So it would just sit there and rot.'

I remembered the abandoned cars being used as goal posts which I had seen on the way through West Belfast.

The biographies of joyriders, she continued, were remarkably similar. 'One, as children, they see other, older ones stealing cars and driving them round and having a great time. Two, they start to burn abandoned cars dumped in their area by other joyriders. Three, older ones who are stealing will give them lifts. They're called "sandbaggers". The security services don't like firing if they see young children in a car. Four, they start to steal themselves, which gives them a sense of pleasure, exhilaration, freedom. Five, finally they break up their stolen cars and sell the parts in the South and realize there's money to be made out of this. That's the moment when they become hooked,' she concluded, which made sense to me, it being the moment money and pleasure came together.

'If you want to help them, and you intervene too early, they think you're stigmatizing them. Enter at the last stage and there's a chance you can get them to realize where this is leading them.'

'Which is?'

'To punishment.'

She inflected the word in a way which gave it a weight of dread. She glanced at Veronica and continued: 'The Provies say joyriding's anti-social, and their attitude's hardening. Years ago, if they caught you, you were humiliated. You were placarded and made to sweep the streets. They went on to tarring and feathering. Then they started kneecapping. First offence, knee or knees. Second offence, ankles, elbows or the knees again. Third offence, you're warned, you've got twenty-four hours to get out or you're shot. Now apparently, with kneecapping not being an effective deterrent any longer, they are bringing in a new one.'

'Oh.'

'Fifty-fifty. You bend over – they shoot you in the spine.'

'So you've a fifty-fifty chance of being paralysed?'

'No. You've a fifty-fifty chance of living.'

'That's a new one,' said Veronica, who had been listening silently so far. 'I know of a boy,' she continued. 'They picked him up. They were going to do him for joyriding. He said to the lads, I'm in my best trousers and my mammy'll kill me if I get a hole in them. Can I go home and change? They said, "Yes." He went home and changed into a pair of old trousers and he came back and they did it.'

'What happened to him?'

'Scraped off the streets.'

'Did he tell the police?'

She looked at me as if I were mad. 'Haven't you seen it written upon gable-ends? *"Informers will die."*'

Mary was staring at me with burning eyes and nodding vigorously. Her nails were bitten to the quick, and her index finger was yellow with nicotine.

'And they just accept it,' she said. 'I can tell you stories like that. A hundred of them.'

Mary again: 'They give them money to buy themselves drink beforehand. They buy a couple of pints of scrumpy and get pissed. Then they're kneecapped. It's terrible when they're brought to hospital. Because they're paralytic, nothing can be done for them, so they just lie there in agony for hours until they sober up.'

Veronica: 'I was in Portadown once, with a young joyrider. We were waiting to go into court. He met another joyrider. They both rolled up their trouser legs and compared their kneecapped knees.'

Mary: 'But the punishment doesn't stop them. For a few hours maybe, while they're in extreme pain, they vow they'll never do it again. But then I've known ones that come out of hospital, and within hours they're back at it, using the crutches to work the pedals.'

Veronica: 'They think, these Provie so-and-so's have done this terrible thing to me. Well, I'll show them. They won't control me. I'm going to steal again. It's the only way they have of striking back.'*

* In his report for the year 1989 the chief constable of the RUC, Hugh Annesley, revealed that the year had seen the highest number of punishment shootings (principally kneecappings) ever carried out in Northern Ireland by the paramilitaries. Police records showed that 161 punishments had been carried out, of which 96 had been by Republicans and 65 by Loyalists. In addition 51 people had been beaten by paramilitaries using a variety of implements such as bars, sticks and concrete blocks. See the *Irish Independent*, 20 July 1989.

Antagonism between the IRA and some joyriders reached such a pitch in 1987 that a group of twenty-one joyriders published a letter in a local West Belfast newspaper declaring they were fed up with the beatings and punishments, and stating they would fight back if the IRA did not stop. See David

THE WORKSHOP

I was not feeling my usual celestial self as I returned to the workshop where I had opted to spend the afternoon. Our subject, to give it its full title, 'Community Liaison: Lay Visitors and Accountability'. There were about a dozen of us.

The session opened with a summary of the situation by a gentleman who wore a fob watch in his breast-pocket. In 1980, he explained, the House of Commons Home Affairs Committee proposed that lay people, drawn from a board, should be able to visit police stations without notice, at any hour of the day or night, and talk to the detainees about their welfare and conditions of detention. The Board of Prison Visitors had been performing a similar function for many years but had no access to those held in police stations. Lord Scarman endorsed the notion in his report on the 1981 Brixton riots, and it is hardly surprising that one of the early pilot schemes was established in Lambeth (which includes Brixton). Six further schemes were established, and subsequently the practice had become widespread. There were now very few areas in which the scheme did not operate. Very few areas in England and Wales, that is.

In Northern Ireland it was different. Although it was rumoured at the time of our workshop that a pilot lay-visiting scheme was underway somewhere in the Province, the current situation was that suspects could be taken into barracks, held for up to seven days under the Prevention of Terrorism Act and not be seen by anybody except a policeman.

*

The chairman pointed to the corner.

'You have some experience in this area, don't you?' he said.

McKittrick, 'Life-and-Death Defiance of Belfast's Joyriders', *Irish Independent*, 15 February 1988.

The woman he addressed had been sitting listening attentively. She had grey hair, watery blue eyes and thin lips. Her name was Margaret O'Donnell, and she was chairperson of the Peace and Reconciliation Group, Derry.

'I do,' she began in a clear, ringing voice, and went on to explain that years before lay visiting had been organized anywhere else, her group had managed to set up an ad hoc system in Derry, whereby its members could visit suspects in the cells of the barracks day or night, talk to prisoners without a policeman present, and in that way ensure that conditions and welfare were up to standard.

*

The room in Stranmillis, where we were sitting, had children's pictures on the walls. The subject was integrated education and attitudes among children to the idea, and while Margaret O'Donnell continued to talk, I looked at them. To me, it seemed, they spoke more eloquently than any statistics of dichotomization. The one right in front of me made a particular impression. It showed two children: one was coloured orange and the other green, and they were separated by a jagged black line.

The population of Northern Ireland is about 35 per cent Catholic and 65 per cent Protestant. The communities may sit side by side on the bus or swim in the same pool, but more often than not they live on separate estates, and go to separate schools and work places; and the make-up of the police is another expression of this separateness. The RUC is overwhelmingly Protestant. In certain areas – West Belfast, where I had seen the arrest earlier in the day – the police are not viewed as part of the community; they are viewed as the enemy, as part of an army of occupation. Members of Nationalist paramilitary groups murder policemen regularly. Mainstream opinion, Protestant and Catholic, Unionist and Nationalist, is horrified by these killings; but this doesn't bring the communities together. Despite the abhorrence among most

Catholics, it remains a fact that they do not join the police; consequently many Protestants suspect that in their heart of hearts all Nationalists hold the police in contempt. What Unionists seem reluctant to take on board is the following: it is dangerous for a Catholic to join the police, and the Catholic who does join must kiss home and family goodbye. He will never live in a Catholic area again, and he must accept that he will be reviled as a traitor by some of his community for the rest of his life.

In addition to this general scenario (applicable throughout Ulster) there was also the matter of Derry's particular circumstances to be considered. The city is 80 per cent Catholic, yet the police are almost all Protestant; inevitably it has become a place of conflict between police and community. Therefore it can only be a good thing that lay visitors are going into the barracks and helping to guarantee the well-being of Catholic suspects, who are thought to be vulnerable in the hands of the police. Furthermore, rather than being a threat to the police, lay visiting has proved to be the opposite: it has led to a decline in the number of allegations, and, consequently, the status of the police has risen.

*

I found myself agreeing with Margaret O'Donnell as she explained her methods.

'I just go to the barracks, say I want to see so-and-so, and say I won't take no for an answer.' And I agreed with her credo. 'I, anyway, do not believe there is such a thing as a legitimate target. I do not want a situation in which every time a policeman hears the dustbin lid rattling outside his back door he has to ask, "Is that the cat or is that someone coming to kill me?" I want justice for them, and I want justice for the detained. Every time someone is harmed by the police, every time a policeman tells a lie, he is harming the police service, and he is harming justice. We must work together against that; we and the police.'

Some of the other members of the workshop, however, were more muted in their response, while the young man in the corner, from West Belfast, in white socks and suede winkle-pickers, said nothing. Finally he was persuaded to speak.

'No, I'm not in favour of lay visiting,' he said.

'Why?'

He wriggled. 'What about my friends, taken into the barracks for joyriding or burglary?' he asked. 'In West Belfast these crimes can earn you a kneecapping from the paramilitaries. And in East Belfast too, for that matter. How can my friends be certain that the lay visitor won't tell the paramilitaries?'

'But we would never tell the paramilitaries who we've seen,' said Margaret O'Donnell. 'Ever.' And then she repeated herself. 'Ever.'

No one in the room doubted this was the truth, and yet the man in the winkle-pickers was adamant: better a hammering in the barracks than the discovery one had been alone with the police, for such a man is vulnerable afterwards to the charge that he has become an informer; and, as the warning goes, written on gable-ends and ghetto walls (and which I was now hearing for the second time that day), '*Informers will die.*'

Lay visiting in Derry, as Margaret O'Donnell repeatedly and correctly insisted, had *never* got anyone into trouble (and detainees also had the right, as she also emphasized, to decline a visit, if they wanted to ensure absolutely their anonymity), but the man in winkle-pickers would not be moved. 'No lay visiting,' he said.

Like the pictures on the walls, this had an eloquence superior to any facts, in this case facts on the grip the paramilitaries exert.

Diary

I agree to meet my friend Norman for a drink. He is a Protestant and lives near the border with Donegal. When I turn up at his house, he says that Wesley, his brother, wants to come along.

We get into the car to drive to their local which is just in the Republic and where IRA men wearing balaclavas and carrying Kalashnikovs had recently kidnapped a customer.

As we drive, Wesley talks cars. 'I have a Citröen like yours in Germany, only it's a diesel,' he says. 'They're so economical, aren't they? One tank does me a whole week of runs in and out of the base, which must be 500 K's all told.'

'K's?'

'Kilometres. Sorry.'

Base? Germany? Then, as we pull into the pub car-park, I notice the tattoo on the back of Wesley's hand, and realize for certain that he is indeed in the British Army. Suddenly I do not want to be in this scene in this film any more. I offer up a prayer as we pass through the saloon door, but then I am dumbfounded, for once we are inside I hear friendly shouts of, 'Hi, Wesley. Hello, Norman,' coming from all sides.

I spend the rest of the evening listening to Norman on the subject of why he is a member of the Orange Lodge [Wesley is somewhere else], while the men at the next table discuss, in graphic detail, their internment in Long Kesh for alleged IRA membership.

23
Reasons to be Cheerful

I

I addressed my letter requesting an interview, not to the Peace and Reconciliation Group, Derry, but to the *Police* and Reconciliation Group. The secretary rang and politely explained I'd made a mistake. 'You know, it wouldn't do for us to be seen as a police and reconciliation group, even though that's an area we're involved in. You understand?'

Despite my *faux pas*, it was agreed that Margaret O'Donnell, the chairperson, would see me.

II

A thumbnail sketch. She is in her early fifties. She was born in Buncrana, Co. Donegal, and came to Derry with her parents when she was eleven. Like so many before him, her father was in search of work. He was not successful, so he went over to Scotland and worked there for the rest of his life. After school Margaret went into nursing, lived in Coventry for a number of years, married in 1961 and came home. Today she lives on the Shantallow Estate with her family, is retired and works full time with the reconciliation group.

What she had – which was the reason I wanted to meet her – was a quality remarkably rare in Northern Ireland: the genuine ability to be even-handed and non-sectarian. 'The police have the hardest job of all to do in this community, and we must help them,' was a phrase she said several times at the conference in Belfast and clearly meant. 'Abuse by the police is absolutely indefensible,' she had said just as often and was equally sincere about.

Listening to her, I thought that here at last was someone who was not partisan; she supported the police, but when they needed to be criticized, she wasn't afraid to do it.

III

The night before I was due to go to Derry, a gale buffeted the house; the windows rattled in their sashes and I could hear the slates which slipped from the roof shattering on the stone flags in the yard. In the morning the radio was full of it; two deaths in England and ninety-mile-an-hour gusts in Antrim. At the end of the news it was mentioned that a youth had been found on the Creggan Estate in Derry that morning, gunshot wounds in his leg, the usual euphemism for a punishment shooting by paramilitaries.

The sun came out, and I set off. Snow on the hills and a miraculous blue sky. In Derry I parked near the Diamond in the city centre, in a street of eighteenth-century houses, and then climbed a flight of rickety stairs to the offices of the Peace and Reconciliation Group. The management committee were meeting, and I was invited to wait in an outer office. I was intrigued by a handwritten notice on the wall:

> What you see here
> What you hear here
> When you leave here
> Let it stay here

'What does that mean?' I asked.

'Sometimes the group will act as a conduit,' said Julie, sitting behind the desk, 'between the paramilitaries and whoever. That is one reason for that. Another is that when young men have been warned they are going to be punished, they come here and we get them off to England. We never talk about this work, and we never keep any files on it.' She shrugged.

'There was a punishment last night,' someone said.

I gathered it wasn't always possible to help.

IV

The management committee meeting finished, and I was invited through. I had expected to see Margaret O'Donnell by herself, but everyone remained around the table.

The group was founded in 1976 and was associated with the Peace People. They have been a completely autonomous body since 1980. Their aim is to improve relations between the communities. To this end they organize a range of activities – sporting, cultural, social – which bring members of the two communities together. They run a minibus which is available to any community organization in the city and which, during the 'no-go' times (when parts of the city were closed to the security services by the paramilitaries), could go into any area. Slightly more contentious has been research mounted by the group into cultural division. This has involved working with antipathetic organizations such as the Derry Apprentice Boys and the Gaelic Athletic Association to create a picture of the common history of the city which will supersede the partial views which pass for history in Northern Ireland.

And then, more contentious still, there is the Police and Public Liaison Committee (PPLC). In the rest of the United Kingdom (and in the Republic for that matter) to sit on such a body signifies simply that one is a good citizen with an interest in public service. Here it means much more: sit on it, and this signifies your support for the police; abstain, and this signifies the reverse. As Sinn Féin have no confidence in the

RUC and support the IRA (whose armed struggle involves shooting members of the RUC), they obviously do not sit. Alas, the SDLP, who dominate Derry City Council, worry that they will lose votes to Sinn Féin if they show the faintest sign of going soft on the RUC – who are still perceived in parts of Derry as a Protestant paramilitary force – and thus the SDLP do not sit either. Obviously Unionists sit, but the police have no interest in a body which is not cross-community; and so, to give the PPLC its cross-community complexion, there is just Margaret O'Donnell and three other members from the voluntary sector.

Because they sit, Margaret and the others are classified in some quarters as 'Castle Catholics' (the term deriving from Dublin Castle, the British administrative centre in Ireland before Partition), meaning they are quislings who co-operate with the British to ensure their system of injustice remains in place. Now one would have thought that using the PPLC to criticize the police when suspects or civilians have been abused or maltreated, and railroading through a system of lay visiting before it came into existence anywhere else (and it was necessary because some suspects were being abused in the barracks in Derry) are most definitely not the actions of collaborators. Unfortunately there are some in Northern Ireland who are surrounded by a carapace of ideology and do not see it like this. The political hardliners describe these benevolent actions as malign or traitorous. Republican paramilitary opinion I can only guess at, but I imagine they have no time for any of this; the conflict between the police and their community is one of the factors which keeps them in business, and they know that whatever helps to heal the rift will therefore be to their disadvantage. However, it also has to be said that there may be a contrast between what the IRA publicly say is not acceptable to them and what they privately allow or even condone.

V

The management committee drifted off. It started pouring with rain outside the office, and a pair of traffic wardens who had been patrolling the area came in to take shelter. Immediately the Visitors' Book came out for them to sign. After one traffic warden had written his name, the second exploded with laughter.

'You can't put yourself down as British,' he said. 'You kick with the wrong foot. You're a Catholic. You can't be a Catholic and British.'

'Why can't I?' the first traffic warden replied.

Here, in a sense, was the whole problem of Northern Ireland in a nutshell. It is hard to be what you want here; rather you are expected to be what you are born.

This was when the phone rang with word that we were to come up to the police barracks.

VI

The barracks was in a street blocked off with concrete barriers which would keep a tank out. We went through a steel gate into the compound. The main building was your classic modern civic construction, *circa* mid sixties to early seventies, concrete, glass, no soul.

We climbed the steps and went into the foyer. On the wall a marble tablet listed the names of all the policemen killed in the Troubles since 1969.

Margaret stopped to look. 'I knew so many of those,' she said. 'Such good men.'

Moments later we were in the waiting-room, a dark cubicle of desperation with graffiti scrawled everywhere.

'Did you see that look?' Margaret nodded towards the blonde girl standing in the foyer. When Margaret had mentioned the good policemen, the girl had given her one of the purest looks of hatred I have seen for a long time. Margaret O'Donnell, like the traffic warden, was paying the penalty of departing from what she was born.

A few minutes later we went upstairs. Officer — had agreed to see me, informally. My questions were careful; his replies were cautious.

'Do you welcome lay visiting?'

'Yes. Obviously it improves relations between police and the community.'

'Would you welcome a statutory system?'

'Yes.'

Our interview meandered on. I wanted to ask about shoot-to-kill and other excesses. Margaret raised these sensitive issues herself. While acknowledging that the police have the hardest job of all, she is also the first to point out their wrongs and isn't coy about listing them, as she then did. Officer — looked uncomfortable, but he took it calmly. This was a conversation between equals. '

Officer — and I returned to batting our diplomatic niceties backwards and forwards. Margaret O'Donnell borrowed a pen and paper, and began writing. It looked like a letter.

Finally I closed my notebook. 'I've got enough,' I said.

Margaret leaned forward to Officer — and gave him the paper. It wasn't a letter; it was a report. Quietly and un-emotionally she stated that the night before a young man had been taken from his car and abused by two policemen. His only crime was to come from a family with paramilitary connections. Officer — blanched; she named the policemen; he promised action. I have no doubt he meant it.

Although this wasn't an official visit, I guess it succeeded for the same reason that the lay visiting succeeded: because trust and confidence existed between the two parties. It also confirmed my belief – contrary to what the man in the winkle-pickers thought – that anything that stops violence is good. The Peace and Reconciliation Group's ad hoc system may be an imperfect way of going about things, and necessarily frail because it is dependent on good-will rather than the rule of the law, but it has to be better than nothing.

VII

We went outside. Night was falling. Margaret O'Donnell offered to guide me through the one-way system and put me on the right road.

'It's raining,' I said, 'I'll bring you home.'

'No. I'll show you the way and you'll let me out at my church.'

It was one of those modern Catholic churches, circular with a conical roof. 'There's a fountain inside,' she said, 'and I look at the water when I pray and it helps to still my mind.'

She went into Our Lady of Lourdes, and I went down the hill on to the new Foyle bridge, a huge curving structure lit up with yellow street-lamps and the dark waters of the river racing below.

Diary

Probably the least-reported fact about the Troubles is the energy Catholics devote to getting their male offspring married as young as possible. It makes sense. With a family they are less likely to join the paramilitaries.

24

Politicians

ANOTHER COUNCIL MEETING

The council chamber in the town hall, Enniskillen: polished tables arranged in a horseshoe; Unionists on one side and Nationalists on the other. The councillors are setting the annual rate.

COUNCILLOR LUNNY: Why must we put up with speeches the length of McCaffrey's?

COUNCILLOR P. MCCAFFREY: At least I didn't scrape in after the tenth or eleventh count.

COUNCILLOR FERGUSON (interrupting the squabbling): Can't this matter be referred back to committee?

COUNCILLOR P. MCCAFFREY: Back to committee? Have you something to hide, Councillor Ferguson, that you won't discuss it in front of us?

COUNCILLOR FERGUSON: You got up to make a point, but you haven't a point to make, so sit down will you?

COUNCILLOR NOBLE (from the Unionist side): McCaffrey, you're just spend, spend, spend. It's a pity we don't have the poll tax looming. That'd stop you in your stride . . .

(The door opens, and the town hall doorman in the town hall blue livery enters, wheeling the tea-trolley.)

COUNCILLOR JOHNSTON (attempting to dampen the sniping): Can I ask councillors to be mindful? There's a man in here writing a book, Mr Gelber [*sic*]; please be mindful.

(Cups of tea are handed round. The tinkling of spoons against china – as the councillors take their sugars – mingles with their voices.)

COUNCILLOR FERGUSON (same subject, different aspect): Let's hope we can look forward to a time when the amenities we provide – the Marble Arch tourist caves, etc. – far from costing the ratepayers anything, will actually contribute to the council budget.

COUNCILLOR P. MCCAFFREY: I see Councillor Ferguson's long-term plan would be to sell off the Marble Arch caves. Well, let me tell him now – hands off! These are not bricks and mortar for the selling. We, as the custodians of the county, must keep them out of the hands of private control.

COUNCILLOR LUNNY: I seem to recall, Councillor McCaffrey, you were originally opposed to the opening of the caves.

COUNCILLOR P. MCCAFFREY: That is a slanderous allegation. Withdraw that or I shall be speaking to my lawyer. Ask him to withdraw – he's a liar.

(Plates of biscuits are passed from hand to hand – one going from Sinn Féin to the Democratic Unionists via the Workers' Party. Sound FX of jam bourbons, coconut whirls and chocolate digestives being crunched up mix with the councillors' voices.)

COUNCILLOR FOSTER (on another subject now): I agree, the new social security regulations about the unemployed having to show they have actively been seeking work will swing hard with them. But what about the other problem: the IRA? They're chasing and frightening work away. The incongruity of it [gesturing towards the Sinn Féin councillors opposite, the proposers of the motion]. They support the armed struggle and the La Mon bombing and the war memorial bombing and the murder of Jillian Johnston here, and of those two unfortunates, Mr Hassard and Mr Love, and yet they talk about unemployment and the evils of the new social security arrangements. They are the evil which must be eliminated. No organization has contributed more to unemployment etc. here than the IRA, whom Sinn Féin support.

COUNCILLOR B. MCCAFFREY: Discrimination and bigotry here provided more unemployment than all the IRA put together. And what about the employment provided by the so-called British security services? Our only intention, which will cause unemployment, is to remove that industry.

(Angry voices fill the council chamber, the individual remarks indecipherable, yet the meaning quite intelligible. Sinn Féin support the IRA in their right to wage war to free Ireland; the Unionists, to put it mildly, do not. The former aspire to an all-Ireland constitutional arrangement; the latter to one in a British context – two positions which I doubt can ever meet, let alone accommodate each other.)

COUNCILLOR FOSTER: Examine your conscience, Councillor B. McCaffrey.

COUNCILLOR B. MCCAFFREY: I don't have to. My conscience is clear, but I'm gagged.

COUNCILLOR FOSTER: Say what you really believe, what your real intentions are.

COUNCILLOR B. MCCAFFREY: Would you like me to disqualify myself from this chamber?

Diary

As a youth, growing up in Enniskillen in the fifties, he joined the IRA and at weekends would go to Galway and Kerry for training. 'We all did,' he explains, 'every one of my friends was involved.' They were only given wooden rifles with which to practise, but, he says, had he been given a real one, he probably would have been stupid enough to have gone North and done something silly with it. Later any chances *of this happening were curtailed when his brother found out what he'd been up to, gave him a thumping and told him to stay home at weekends.*

However, the innocence of those days, he continues angrily, has given way to something much less innocent by early 1990, which is when we are talking. The last Protestant on his estate, he tells me, and a part-time UDR member, has just left. A bomb had been placed under his car. He is disgusted with this action committed, as he sees it, in his name, yet how can he object? 'You think it's the poor soldiers are terrorized by the IRA? Or the Protestants are terrorized by them? Wrong. The Catholics are the ones they really terrorize. We're their victims.'

After some minutes of denunciation his feelings are assuaged, and he offers me a cup of tea.

PART FOUR

SPRING

25
The Architect

There was to be an addition to the Enniskillen war memorial to commemorate the eleven people killed in the bombing. A local architect, Richard Pierce, was commissioned to do the design. I was with him on his first day of work.

*

'The fact I have undertaken to do this job,' he said, as we sat at the table in his living-room, 'will be seen by some of my neighbours as an act of collusion with the enemy. I am taking sides, as they see it, by what I am doing. But what can I do? My concern is with my neighbours on both sides of the divide, and it is my hope that these eleven people did not die in vain. This addition to the war memorial has to be an act of reconciliation.'

He opened his well-thumbed *History of Architecture on the Comparative Method* at the entry on Whitehall in London.

'As you can see,' he continued, pointing at the photograph of Lutyens's Cenotaph, 'this is an absolutely marvellous piece, which falls between architecture and sculpture. Lutyens was designing beautiful simple shapes in stone when he did this, and that is what I hope I will be doing.'

He drew the shutters and turned on the slide projector. On the wall fell huge images of Gaudi's Sagrada Familia, the great cathedral in Barcelona.

'It may all be done in stone,' said Richard, pointing at a detail of animals seeming to emerge from stone, 'but it looks more like ice-cream, doesn't it? My idea for the war memorial here is to have eleven doves in Portland stone rising round the feet of the Unknown Soldier. But to work, these must have something of the same quality as Gaudi's birds and animals.'

He opened the shutters, flooding the room with light, laid a piece of tracing paper on his drawing board and sharpened a pencil. 'This is the moment when I should say a prayer,' he said.

'What size would these doves be?' I wondered.

'I'd leave that to the sculptor. I have one in mind incident-ally, Philip Flanagan. It would be nice if he did it, not only because he's extremely good but because he's a Catholic and I'm from the Prod side.'

Slowly he started to sketch, and on the tracing paper the first dove began to appear.

'Of course the committee are going to have to decide whether it's going to be eleven doves or twelve,' he continued quietly. 'They'll have to decide if Ronnie Hill gets up there or not. He's been in a coma since it happened, technically he's alive, but ah . . .' His voice trailed away.

'Are the names going on the apron?' I asked, pointing on the drawing to the canopy of stone that lies around the foot of the Enniskillen war memorial.

'No, the frost would destroy them there. They'll go on the side . . . the side nearest where they died . . . and the wording will start, "In memory of our neighbours", or something like that. There are some people who are so embittered that they might like to have "Murdered by Catholics" or "Killed by terrorists", but ah . . .' His voice trailed off for a moment, as letters started to form at the end of his pencil, and then returned. 'I've just reread the parable of the Good Samaritan, and we could do with some of that here; just substitute Protestant or Catholic – whatever you're not – for Samaritan, and you'll get my message.' Another lacuna and then he said, 'The IRA killed their neighbours, which wasn't very Samaritan-like . . .'

He pointed with his pencil at the words he had drawn and

repeated, 'In memory of our neighbours who died near this spot.' He then continued, 'And apart from that we'll have just their names and the date, and I think we'll make them alphabetical. That way we keep the husbands and wives together, which is poignant.'

Half an hour later and the drawing was completed. It showed the apron of Portland stone with the existing pedestal resting on top. On top of this Richard had added the block with the doves emerging from the stone, and above stood the Unknown Soldier. It was very simple, clean and elegant, and no doubt it would have pleased Sir Edwin Lutyens.

Diary

'I don't know what to vote when the elections come round. I'm not on either side. I'm English and outside all of this.'

The woman – a resident of Ulster all her life – and I are sitting in her conservatory. Mrs Brown has blue eyes and broken veins in her cheeks. She says 'darling' often, like an old-time actress from rep. She reads Horse and Hound *and the* Field. *She is a widow.*

'We've had this going on for 500 years, these troubles, and the funny thing is, everyone knows how to solve the problem except the Ulster people themselves. I wonder to myself sometimes if they don't actually want them.'

Mary, thirty-something, appears with a tray of coffee and biscuits.

'Would you get on with the windows?' says Mrs Brown.

'Is that wise?' asks Mary. 'It looks like it's going to rain.'

'Oh, no, battle on, battle on,' insists Mrs Brown.

'She can do everything for herself, you know,' Mary whispers to me as she passes. 'She just has me up for the company, really.'

As soon as Mary closes the door, Mrs Brown taps my arm and says, 'It's not just for company. I also have her up so I have someone with whom I can go on little excursions.' And then she adds, 'She thinks I'm deaf, but I hear everything perfectly clearly.'

26

First Moderate

I

We met in his small and, on that day, freezing office. The walls were painted the colour of Germolene. The shelves were filled with dusty law books. Raymond Ferguson, the Unionist leader on the council, sat behind a desk piled with dog-eared files, papers, pens and pencils. He was a man of about fifty with very blue eyes, a barrel-shaped chest and enormous hands. As he spoke, he touched the tips of his fingers together.

'What do you feel about the council meetings?' I asked to begin.

'I regard them as extremely important as a contact point. At the meetings I meet people whom, as a Unionist, one doesn't usually meet. In Enniskillen, in the class I'm in, there are Roman Catholic people, but I often wonder what's going on among the other social classes. And that's what I find out at the meetings, and it's a sobering experience listening to Sinn Féin. What I learn from the meetings is that the IRA are genuine. But when I'm in there, I'm thinking to myself, how am I going to handle this?'

'How do you?'

'You can't argue with their views rationally. I don't want to sound sinister here, by the way.'

He gave me a look so that I did not misunderstand. He was not recommending the irrational route, i.e., assassination.

'They're so imbued with their sense of grievance and their sense of place here in Ireland and their ideas of "National sovereignty". They're convinced that they are the original and rightful occupants of the land. They don't want intruders

178

to feel unwelcome, but they do want them to know they're here on the sufferance of the Gaelic descendants represented by Sinn Féin.

'It's a racist code essentially. It will not survive two, three or four generations. In time, as our civilization develops, young people will turn away from this narrow, inward-looking ideology and out towards the country and Europe. But this is not to say they won't certainly always have a loyalty to their place of origin. However, that loyalty won't develop a philosophy which says "Ourselves Alone".'

From here the conversation turned to de Valera.

'He believed in the natural Irishman, you know, hanging over the hearth door, agrarian, pastoral, living in a rural paradise, Roman Catholic and exclusive. It was de Valera who established the trade barriers and declined to pay the land annuities – the payments owing to the British government for estates which had been bought for the tenantry in the nineteenth century under the Gladstone administration. He engineered it so that his country became small and inward-looking. Irish neutrality was part of the same "Ourselves Alone" philosophy. You could argue that it was all a natural reaction to the previous British colonial presence, and that the Irish were properly entitled to do what they did once they got power. Okay.

'Anyhow, the result was terrible poverty; he made the conditions in the country worse than they would normally have been. And the Irish never came to terms with their problems, really, until the Whitaker report* in 1958, which recommended opening the country up to trade and so forth.

'Today, that tendency to be inward-looking and anti-English, I think it's all going in the South really; it exists only along the border because there is still a presence "up here" to feel antagonistic towards.'

---

* On economic development.

II

'What about civil rights? Do you think those involved had genuine grievances?' I asked next.

'Of course they did. Houses were on a spoils system. If there was a Protestant council, Protestants got the houses, and if there was a Catholic council, Catholics got them – that would be in places like Newry and Mourne. But the point is, gerrymandering had seen to it that there weren't that many Roman Catholic councils.

'However, if you'd been a fly on the wall at a Unionist meeting at the time, you'd have heard all the older generation saying, "Why is everyone so opposed to gerrymandering? We get in where we're in the majority and we give our people houses, and 'they' get in where they're in the majority and they give their people houses. This is politics, isn't it?"

'So it wasn't Stormont that civil rights was against, it was local government, and specifically within local government what they were complaining about was the property vote. Of course, at the time we're speaking of, back in the sixties, the Unionists were simply applying a system that had obtained in England up to 1947 when Clement Attlee abolished the property vote.'

'None the less, you would agree the civil rights protesters had valid grievances?'

'Definitely. There were grievances which required redressing, and Stormont did redress them all, but the movement didn't stop there.'

III

'What do you feel about a United Ireland?' I asked.

'Because of what I feel, a lot of people think that I'm not a Unionist any more. What I feel is that the politics need to be sorted out on the island of Ireland by the people of Ireland.

The government in Westminster doesn't care. It looks on this as a sort of white man's burden. The Unionist people don't want a United Ireland. They're suspicious of the Republic. They fear that if there were a 32-county Republic in which they would be in the minority, there would be a certain amount of evening up, which would be to their disadvantage, evening up by the Catholic population, that is. I don't think it would happen, but the fear is there. And this is the sort of thing that people fight for.

'My fears are not about the South in general (except of course from those who live along the border) but about those Roman Catholics in the North with an axe to grind. The people who voted Sinn Féin and supported the IRA.

'The only solution is some sort of federation, and if you read the 1920 Government of Ireland Act you can see that was implicit. What the British government did in a sense was to set up a federal Ireland, which is what we have now, with a Council of Ireland to mediate between the two. A great idea abandoned first by the Dáil and then by Stormont. That was part of the process by which we grew apart and became paranoid about each other.

'The situation today is that the South have become a good bit more sane and balanced about us; on the other hand, the North have remained as paranoid as they always were towards them.

'At the end of the day the whole thing is a matter of symbols, and the settlement will be over symbols. What are we going to do about the Union Jack, for instance? Will it be accepted in the South? I suppose Protestants accepted – that is Protestants who were south of the border after Partition – that the Union flag wouldn't fly any more. Perhaps they'll accept that up here one day as well. But when these things go, people feel threatened, and when they feel threatened, they go out and buy guns and we don't want that, do we?

'Another problem is that we have two different financial systems. Here every man, woman and child is subsidized to the tune of, say, £1,000 per year by central government.'

'But if there were to be a United Ireland tomorrow,' I interrupted, 'and everyone here was told, by the way, there's going to be a drop in living standards – you're all going to be £1,000 a year worse off, no one would wear it.'

'No, they wouldn't. As part of our agreement with the South there would have to be an understanding with Britain whereby the subvention would continue. It would be a hell of a risk, of course. And for ten years – or however long this subvention was going to go on being paid – we would have to work very hard to ensure that we had sufficient wealth to fill the gap when the subvention was eventually withdrawn.'

'People here know, don't they, that the wealth that they have is coming from the United Kingdom?'

'Of course they do, and this explains why Sinn Féin aren't doing so well.'

'So it's economics and not revulsion that drives people away from Sinn Féin?'

'It would be here, yes. If you look at the Sinn Féin supporters we have in Fermanagh, they live along the border, they regard themselves as native Irish, they're farming people, and they're essentially very conservative in their political and economic outlooks. They have absolutely no truck with the international socialist outlook of the Sinn Féin in Belfast. Do you remember when they got abortion through at the *Ard-Fheis*, and the rural membership were so horrified it was thrown out the next year?'

'Meantime, what happens here?'

'It'll tick on. I don't see any big changes. There's no movement within the Unionist camp. The changes, when they come, will be economic; they'll be gradual; they'll be non-political.'

Diary

'*One of the people on our books here is a painter,*' says the community worker in charge of the scheme for placing the long-term unemployed.

'*You may remember last summer was one of the best we've had for a long time, and we had a lot of work over in Derrychara, which as you know is a Protestant estate. So we got a gang together and sent them off, but one man wouldn't go.*

'*And he wouldn't go and he wouldn't go and he wouldn't go, and eventually the point was reached when I had to say to him, "Look, unless you go and do the work, I'm going to have to fire you."*

'*So he undid his shirt right there and then, and he showed me his chest, and there, tattooed in the middle, were two tricolours and the message "Born 1969".*

'*I understood at once that he couldn't possibly go to Derrychara with that on his chest, especially in the hot weather. Eventually he would have to take off his shirt and what was on his chest would have caused a riot.*'

27

Second Moderate

1

A house on an estate outside Enniskillen. In the living-room there was an electric fire and a pile of women's magazines. I noticed *Options* and *Prima*. It was the house of Davy Kettyles. As we spoke, his fringe kept falling over his eyes. His first child slept in a carry-cot in the corner.

It is as well to get these matters out of the way. Davy Kettyles is Catholic. In his family his father did not vote, and his mother, he thought, voted SDLP.

He was a teenager in the early seventies, when this round of the Troubles was at its worst. It was relatively peaceful in Fermanagh, but the disturbances elsewhere were on television every night. As was inevitable, given his background, civil rights caught his attention. His attitudes hardened, and he began to identify with the Nationalist movement.

In 1975 he joined the Workers' Party.* There was some logic to this, given their involvement in civil rights, but it was also a little illogical, given his ultra attitudes. It was not long before, as he put it, he was taken aside and 'given a good talking to' by some of the other members. The party had just been through extraordinary convulsions, in the process of which it had undergone a transformation from being the political wing of the Official IRA into being a socialist party against terrorism and committed to democracy.†

* Known then as Official Sinn Féin in the South and Republican Clubs in Northern Ireland.
† The name change – the last stage in the process of becoming a democratic party – came in 1982, the same year that the party's three TDs supported Charles Haughey as taoiseach and enabled him to form a government.

His colleagues put it to him that either he improve his analysis of Ireland and recognize the situation was more complex than the verities of Nationalism had previously led him to think, or acknowledge that he had in fact joined the wrong party and depart for Sinn Féin. Kettyles stuck it out.

Later he moved to London and became a postman.

'I used to play cards a lot at work,' he said, 'and every time a black player left, the whites would pass remarks, and I'd be sitting there listening and I'd think to myself, I wonder what they say about me, a Paddy, when I get up to leave.'

He returned to Enniskillen in 1980. He became reinvolved with the Workers' Party and worked at the Welfare Rights Centre, advising on state entitlements and benefits.

In the 1988 local government elections, when Sinn Féin dropped from eight seats to four on the council, he was elected. His ward stretches from the Catholic Kilmacormick Estates in Enniskillen to Lisbellaw, a Loyalist village.

According to the exit polls which the party conducted, of the 1,150 votes he received, about 40 per cent were from Loyalist people against about 60 per cent from Nationalists.

He is today the youngest councillor in the chamber.

II

'The council meetings get pretty noisy sometimes, don't they?' I began.

'Oh, yes, but some of the members have admitted to me, all the shouting and barracking that goes on, it's just a game, and they deliberately mislead their supporters about the cordiality which they have for each other.'

'Who said this to you?'

'One or two of the Unionists. I don't go along with any of that, by the way, particularly here in Northern Ireland, where that kind of posturing is actually dangerous and may cost lives.'

'How do you find your colleagues?'

'I think the most important thing we have to do is to encourage the young to enter into the process. People may not like politicians, but if you don't have politicians, you end up with dictators. You must get in there in order to register your conviction.'

'But there's no incentive to get in, is there? The councillors have no power, and there is no change.'

'I don't entirely agree with that, but I recognize it's bad. Voting here is by tribe, that's why there's no change. Voting for a candidate isn't positive but negative. You're not voting to put someone in; you're voting to keep someone out. You're voting to keep them out regardless of the quality or calibre of who it is that you're putting in.'

'What can the Workers' Party offer?'

'You mean in terms of power and achievement? We've won some campaigns, but we don't have any illusions. We're small.'

'You rather disturb some of the other councillors.'

'Oh?'

'Any idea why?'

'I suppose what they see is a small party which suddenly got 13 per cent of the vote – which they had always thought was impossible – and the fact that we're a class-based party must also make them nervous.

'If you look at Sinn Féin's voters here in Fermanagh, for instance, if they were in the South they'd all be natural Fianna Fáil voters. And Fianna Fáil have little identification with socialism.

'And Sinn Féin don't have much to do with it either,' he continued, 'despite what Gerry Adams and Danny Morrison and the rest of them say. I once caught a man who supported Sinn Féin coming through a picket line, and he had a James Connolly badge on. He wasn't a socialist – obviously, otherwise he wouldn't have been going through a picket line – and he was wearing this badge because he thought Connolly was a great Republican hero who'd fought at the GPO.

'I'm Republican, but I've given up arguing that I'm one. The word has been absolutely destroyed by the Nationalists, just like the Ceauşescus of this world have absolutely debased the word "communist".'

'What does Republican mean to you?'

'Republicans were originally non-sectarian and aspired to a single nation which would include Catholics, Protestants and Dissenters. That was nearly 200 years ago. It degenerated after that into sectarianism.

'But today we in the Workers' Party have moved forward into class politics. Those who want to maintain seventeenth-century politics still dominate, however. There's still extra-ordinary bitterness here, and it's all related to the land. That's why you get things like the Provos killing boys knowing full bloody well they left the UDR ten years ago, but they kill them because they know that once they're dead, there'll be no one else left to take the farm over, and it'll have to be sold to a Catholic. It's as naked as that.'

III

'What would you think about forcibly integrating the schools?' I asked.

'Oh, no, you've got to allow people the right to educate their children the way they want to have them educated. If we had forcible integration here, the Roman Catholic Church would go nuts. It would be the crusades all over again. They'd be hopping up and down on the spot, demanding their Southern rights, and they'd be applying blackmail to the parents.'

IV

'What will happen here?'

'I've given up predicting. I think the Provos are out anyway. At least they were out, and then they hijacked the civil rights movement, and they were back, and then it looked like they were down and out again, and then up came the hunger strike, and wallop, they were back in the saddle. I think their bubble has burst again now. I think at the moment we're in a vacuum, and in this vacuum the *status quo* rules the roost.'

'Do you see yourselves as the inheritors of the mantle of 1916?'

'Oh, no, not at all, we're democratic socialists. We don't support terrorism. We've grown up in a way in which Sinn Féin haven't. They actually think to themselves, this is Namibia, this is South Africa, this is Palestine, here in Northern Ireland. It's not. What the civil rights movement set out to achieve, it achieved. It achieved its basic conditions, housing, one man one vote, disarming the police, and so on.'

'Yes, the police were disarmed, but now they're armed again,' I said. 'That was a lost opportunity, wasn't it?'

'Absolutely, but one has to accept that Westminster also had some part to play in it all. The things they did were so stupid. Bloody Sunday, the West Belfast curfew – they played absolutely into the hands of the Provos.

'But I think the situation here now has cooled down somewhat, and some of those in Sinn Féin have come to realize they've been conned.

'We're a working-class party, and we've been through struggles, and we've seen there's no place for dogma. If Marx were living, he might very well rewrite what he wrote. Marx said, didn't he, don't call me a Marxist. And he rewrote sections of *Das Kapital* after the Paris Commune. No dogma, no fundamentalism, nothing written in stone – I don't want hell on earth but a situation where people can live better and influence their destiny.'

Diary

He is an old farmer and an ex-B-Special, now in the UDR. He has been a member right from the moment the regiment was founded.

'Why do you serve?' I ask.

Back comes the reply, quick as a flash, 'To keep Ulster British.'

He is retiring in a week's time. A string of stories follow about Owen Carron, Bobby Sands's agent, sometime MP for the constituency of Fermanagh–South Tyrone; arrested January 1986 on a firearms charge and given bail to fight the local Westminster election, he went on the run and was subsequently rearrested in the Republic in February 1988.

I make notes. The account is extraordinary and, I realize, for security reasons, unprintable.

Beyond the bay window of his living-room dusk is falling. We smoke.

'Are you ever at risk, here, at home?' I ask.

'Here's the boy'll protect me,' he says.

He pulls his personal security weapon from his belt and waves it at me. He is never without it, ever.

'Do you want to see the thingamy I check under the car and the tractor with for bombs?' he inquires.

I demur. I remember seeing something that did this job – a mirror on a stick – in the bad old days of the Cold War, travelling between East and West Germany. So to pass the time he takes me on an imaginary tour of his farm. We take in mined culverts, gates booby-trapped with grenades, trip wires to nail bombs. Yet he is not frightened. He loves the service. Why else does he stay in the job beyond the retirement age?

And once a month he collects his pay and drinks it with his friends in the pub.

28

Borderland

The traveller to Fermanagh, if he turns into the village of
Derrylin, will find it consists of a single street spread out over
half a mile, with the occasional tricolour or black flag flying
from a lamp-post. The only sign of Protestantism is the tiny
Church of Ireland church on the outskirts, alone and iso-
lated.

Heading out of the village and in the direction of the
'unapproved crossing' to Ballyconnell, the traveller will find
himself on a stretch of road locally known as 'bomb alley',
and he will notice that the hedgerows and the fields, instead of
being the usual lush green associated with Ireland, are coated
with a fine white dust.

The explanation for this will appear after a mile or two,
when he will see, looming on his right, a quarry, various
works for making tiles and T-bars, and an enormous cement
factory, a towering construction of smoking pipes and chim-
neys which sits on top of a hill.

II

The owner of it all is Sean Quinn – a name one sees on the
sides of lorries all over Ireland – whose story has a classic
trajectory. In 1973 he inherited the 23-acre farm on which his
works currently stand. There was gravel on the land, which
he started to sell. Later, benefiting from the early Thatcher
years when there was a 100 per cent tax-free allowance on

reinvested profits, he diversified into concrete blocks and tiles. Today he is described as a Thatcherite miracle in bandit country (he is only a mile from the border). Something like 60 per cent of his business is in the South, and about 40 per cent of his workforce are from the South. His factory supplies around 22 per cent of the market, North and South. He employs only a few Protestants, because, as he explained in a recent interview, 'there weren't very many in the area'.*

Although his mother still lives by the factory, Sean Quinn has moved three miles away into the Republic, and, furthermore, his impressive diversification into pubs and hotels is confined to the Republic. He now plays the stock market with a London broker. He is in his forties.

*

I went to meet Sean Quinn. He was a large man with what can properly be described as twinkling blue eyes. We met in his works canteen, a small room with a worktop and a sink and smelling faintly of washing-up liquid; it was where his employees ate their lunch.

He openly admitted to being a Nationalist and was adamant that he didn't supply the security services (despite their hunger for building supplies because of the enormous ongoing programme for the refurbishment of police barracks). However, at the end of the day, it's the staggering sight of Sean Quinn's empire straddling this stretch of the border that sticks in the memory, not his political allegiance.

III

It was arranged for me to go out with one of Quinn's drivers. Joe Heaney was a Dubliner who drove a bus in London for

* Colm Tóibín, *Walking along the Border*, p. 88.

ten years. After marriage and the birth of his four children, his wife, a native of Co. Cavan, demanded that they return home to her people's place – twenty acres of 'bad land' and five poor milking cows. They came back to desperate conditions; an uncongenial rural life which both did not pay and lacked the excitement of the city. It was hard going, until Joe Heaney got a job driving a lorry for Sean Quinn.

*

It was raining that morning as we ran across the car-park and climbed into Joe Heaney's dumper truck. Then we bumped round to the quarry behind. Here, in every direction in which I looked, there were stones. They were being washed and sorted into their various sizes and tumbled from conveyor belts to form huge piles.

A load was dumped into the back, and we drove on to the main road, heading for the border. In the cab, the windscreen wipers clacking backwards and forwards and hot air rushing from the de-mister, we smoked, and I asked what he felt about the soldiers.

He felt sorry for them, he said, adding that on the whole relations between the drivers and the military were good. It was only when a new regiment came on and they wanted to throw their weight around a bit to establish themselves that tension mounted.

'And what about the regiment that's on now?'

'Oh, they've been here for months. No problems,' he said.

We passed a thatched cottage – one of the few left in the county – which crouches in the shadow of Quinn's state-of-the-art cement works, and rolled to a halt a couple of hundred yards further on in front of the VCP. It was pretty much like all the VCPs along the border – a construction of concrete and steel painted with camouflage colours. There was a traffic light at the front glowing red, and on the wall beside it a notice:

We apologize for the
inconvenience caused.
Please do not blame us.
Blame the TERRORISTS.

Every vehicle which goes in and out of Northern Ireland along this road has to pass through here. Once inside the VCP the vehicle may be photographed secretly. A record of the registration number is made. The driver is often interviewed by a soldier. There are permanent VCPs all along the border between the Republic and Northern Ireland, and their purpose is to funnel all the traffic coming in and out. They are the front line of the fight against terrorism.

The traffic light turned green, and we edged forward, slipping under the barrier which can be dropped when the army want to trap vehicles inside, and bumping over the sleeping policemen laid across the road.

In the middle of the VCP, in what in effect was a chamber which it was impossible to see into from outside, a military policeman was standing by the pillbox. He saw Joe, recognized him, and with a smile waved us on.

On the other side we were now in a no man's land, the part of the North between the VCP and the actual border. This narrow strip is said to be one of the principal places of confrontation between the IRA and the security services. However, this afternoon, in the sheeting rain, it looked perfectly normal.

It is also a place of business, and there were two garages by the roadside, erected to take punts off the Southerners who flooded over to avail themselves of the cheap petrol in the North.

'Will you look at that,' said Joe, pointing at a lorry container, minus its wheels, which had been beached between the first and second garages.

'The man in the first garage – the one closest to the border – dumped that there, you know why?'

I did not.

'So drivers coming up from the South wouldn't see the second garage, because it blocked the view, and would pull into his garage even if there was a queue at his pumps. It's a fierce business, making money. Now that house,' he continued, pointing at a long cottage by the side of the road. 'The border runs right through the middle. Two old boys lived in there. They watched television in the South but went to bed in the North.'

A few yards later a rusting notice loomed up in the middle of the road saying, 'Irish Customs Post'. Joe explained the situation quickly. There is no UK customs post on the Fermanagh side (it would get blown up if there were), so the arrangement that Quinn's have come to is that all forms are left at the Republic's post, and they sort out the paperwork both for themselves and the UK. Otherwise every driver would have to go to Enniskillen to sort out his paperwork before he could go South, and that would make business absolutely impossible to conduct.

Joe Heaney pulled up and hopped out, saying, 'Got to get the docket stamped.'

He ran through the rain and into the hut. No Quinn driver ever fails to deal with his paperwork, he had told me, a situation many a haulage company would envy. But then Quinn's employees are paid on a completely different basis from most haulage company employees. They do not receive salaries. They are paid according to their productivity: literally, how many loads they shift. And if the paperwork isn't done, all dockets signed, and so on, no pay-cheque at the end of the week. The tabloid sobriquet, a Thatcherite miracle in bandit country, was not so far off the mark.

Joe Heaney rushed back. 'All done,' he shouted.

As he clambered into the van, a slew of cars travelling North to South appeared as if from nowhere and hurtled past.

'Do you see them?' he asked. 'They wait up the road and then when one of our lorries is parked here, which is when they know the customs men can't see the road, they all hurry past.'

'They use you as a screen for smuggling?'

'I suppose you could look at it like that.'

He put the truck into gear, and we drove off to dump the stones at the new hotel Sean Quinn was building at Bally-connell.

Diary

A chance conversation in a pub. As we talk about a United Ireland, he keeps slipping into sexual metaphors.

The Protestant community in the North is the virgin bride. She is a bit nervous, but once she is over the first night she will see the light, and she will be mad for it after that. And then the island of Ireland will be one, and everything in the garden will be rosy.

At the end I am left wondering, is our national aspiration sometimes not the cover for a rape fantasy?

29

South of the Border

I

It was still dark at six in the morning when we left. Outside
Richard's car windows the rounded shapes of Fermanagh
rolled by – hills and dips and more hills – it was like driving
past an endless roller-coaster.

I asked about his family genealogy. Richard's maternal
grandfather was Scottish, and his grandmother was from
Liverpool. They married (before the First World War) and
came to Co. Wexford, where grandfather worked as head
gardener on a large estate.

'In those days before Partition,' observed Richard, 'the
landlords liked to give their head positions to Protestants, and
if possible to English ones. So, often you would find in country
houses that the head butler, the head gardener, and so on,
would be English. The rest would be Catholic. Grandfather
was Scottish, which I suppose was the next-best thing.'

Then came the Troubles, which were followed by the
withdrawal of the British administration from the South. Out
went the old order and in came the new. Richard's grandparents were now Protestants in the wrong place at the wrong
time. Grandfather was 'advised' by the IRA to leave.

The family came North, to Florence Court, seat of the Cole
family and original founders of Enniskillen, bringing with
them a daughter who went on to become one of the best
music teachers the county has known.

Roll forward to 1935, George V's Jubilee. Four representatives were selected from Fermanagh to sing in a choir in the
Albert Hall in honour of the King. The alto was the music

teacher and the tenor a man called Bertie Pierce, from Enniskillen, and a partner in a long-established building contracting firm. Although they had never met before, the alto and the tenor had both heard of each other. In London they fell in love; they married and their middle child was Richard, sitting beside me at the wheel.

II

Richard has an architectural practice; he is also the inspector of churches for the Church of Ireland Diocese of Clogher. The parochial boundaries pre-dated Partition by about 1,000 years, and so the bishop's domain is on both sides of the border. Every church has to be inspected every five years, and I was accompanying Richard to have a look at four, all in the Republic.

A couple of miles north of the border, near Rosslea, a red light suddenly showed palely just a few yards ahead. As he slammed on the brakes, Richard's arm came down like a railway gate to prevent my heading through the windscreen. Seconds later we stopped just a few inches short of the soldier who had leapt out of the ditch to flag us down.

Richard wound down his window and a boot-polish-covered face with two shining eyes in the middle stared in. 'We nearly had you then, you know,' Richard said. It was a genial remonstration. 'We were almost on you before we saw the light.'

The soldier smirked and shrugged. Now that my eyes had adjusted, I could see the other members of this mobile patrol, the foliage stuck into the webbing of their tin helmets wobbling as they moved.

'Any identification?' the soldier asked with a strong Scottish accent, apparently indifferent to his brush with death.

At the Derryard checkpoint a couple of miles further on, we relayed what had just happened. Another boot-polish-covered face nodded and spoke, Scottish again, 'If ye had run him down, ye might have been doin' us all a favour.'

Grim laughter from the shadows, where figures crouched with their guns. Two men from this regiment, the King's Own Scottish Borderers, had been killed by the IRA in this check-point just before Christmas.

'Identification, please,' said the figure at the window.

For the second time in five minutes Richard showed his driving licence, and the soldier scrutinized our faces. It was an odd situation, I thought. Richard's ancestors had been driven from the South by the spiritual ancestors of the IRA men these soldiers were seeking. And that, in its turn, was connected to why we were going there.

One direct consequence of that mass exodus of Protestants from the South to the North in the years immediately after Partition – an exodus in which Richard's family were simply one small statistic – was a decline in the size of the Protestant congregations. They shrank, with the result that the church buildings suffered, and it was about these that Richard would be making recommendations in the reports he would eventually compile as a result of his inspections.

III

We reached our first church, St Maeldoid's in the parish of Mucknoe, near Castleblayney, Co. Monaghan. We turned through gates and in the half-light I saw another car was parked in the drive.

'Mr Smythe has already arrived,' I heard Richard saying.

This was the rural dean, the overseer of these so-called quinquennial inspections. 'He's English,' Richard added.

'How did he end up here?'

'God sent him,' said Richard, and with that he climbed out and I followed.

One has a certain expectation about Protestant clergymen

at the Anglican end of the spectrum; one expects them to be eccentric, odd, not of this world; and as soon as I saw Mr Smythe, I knew that I was not going to be disappointed.

Mr Smythe wore a Russian fur hat; but he also wore a Parker jacket of the kind sported by Mods in the sixties. On his left breast there was a St Albans flash and a Union Jack; on his right a Drumbeggan flash (Drumbeggan, Co. Cavan, is Mr Smythe's parish) and the Irish tricolour. He had a trim dark beard with flecks of grey in it and thick lips. He looked serious and moody and Old Testament, but he also looked, well, faintly comical; a dog-collar-wearing Mod with contradictory emblems on his coat from two countries which have been continuously in conflict for the last 700 years. If he'd come on a Vespa, I wouldn't have been surprised.

We retreated from the freezing wind into the church, which was even colder than it had been outside. Richard immediately began to scour the place for signs of rot, enemy of every church, and, judging by the smell, a particular enemy of this one. A floorboard groaned beneath him, and he shouted out, 'Sometimes my seventeen stone can be useful. Yes, there's definitely a bit of rot here.'

Our party had now been joined by the rector, an Ulsterman with a nice but set smile and even teeth, and two church wardens: Mr Higgins was thin and well-groomed; his colleague, in contrast, whose name I never got, was a plump latter-day Somerville and Ross character, with wild, tousled hair, a leather car coat which was balding at the elbows and a copy of a racing paper sticking jauntily out of his back pocket.

I took a quick look around. On the table, near the baptismal font, books of Common Prayer with black warped covers and damp pages were piled beside collection boxes for the Mothers' Union Overseas Fund and the Christian Missionary Society. On the wall above a memorial to those who died in the Great War. At the front memorials to faithful land agents, placed by the local landowners, the Blayneys. Anglican churches never fail to act as a sort of small-town *Debrett's*, providing the

outsider with a crash course on *Who's Who* or *Who Was Who*
locally.

'What happened to the Blayneys?' I addressed the question
to Mr Higgins, as we watched Richard disappear up a creak-
ing ladder to examine the entablature above a column.

'Oh, the Land Acts of 1920 something,' he said gloomily.
'All their land was taken. They took off to England.'

He refolded his arms and sighed as we stared at the pews
stretching away from us.

'This would have been full in those days.'

'You mean hundreds?'

Mr Higgins nodded. 'Maybe.'

'And now?'

'We had twenty-four in last Sunday.'

The operatic form of the inspector of churches descended
the ladder, and Mr Higgins led me off to see the brass plates
on the pews which earmarked them as the seat of this big
estate or that one. Then Mr Higgins led me into the vestry to
view the engraving of Lord Cadwallader (the Blayney title, if
I'm not mistaken) which hung there. As I contemplated this
gentleman (he was the fifth lord), bewigged and stern faced,
and as I read below of his various military ranks in the British
Army and of the numerous positions he had held on behalf of
the Crown in the county – sheriff, lord lieutenant, justice of
the peace – I felt as if I had left Ireland and had been
transported to somewhere in Eastern Europe (pre-Gorbachov,
of course), and that an old retainer was giving me a privileged
glimpse of the relics of the *ancien régime* which had survived
the rapacious Communists.

'The fifth lord built this church, and he gave the land for
the Catholic church besides us,' said Mr Higgins. 'Did you
notice it on the way in?'

I had indeed; it was on the adjacent lot; neat and clean and
without a spire.

'The fifth lord, when he gave the Catholics that land,'
continued Mr Higgins, 'put in the agreement that they

couldn't have a bell in a tower. There was a bell in here, and he said the one bell would do for the whole parish.'

'They agreed?'

'Yes, but they put the bell up anyhow.'

'Oh.'

'He'd only said they couldn't have one inside. He hadn't said they couldn't have it outside, like they have on the scaffold by the gate, had he?'

Was this a folk tale which proved that Catholics are wily and not to be trusted? Or did it say that the English in Ireland are always doomed to get things wrong because of their literal-mindedness? It was both, I decided, and realized I had left Eastern Europe, which had some verities at least, and was back in my own country, which seemed to specialize in the creation of stories which can sustain contradictory points of view.

IV

Two more churches and it was lunch-time. Richard parked his car in front of a field full of muddy animals, and we ate tangerines and brown bread, while the windows slowly misted. Beside us Mr Smythe sat in his car, reading a missionary journal.

'Let's get on,' Richard said, and we got out.

The next thing that happened, I am not quite certain how, was that Mr Smythe gathered I was on the other side of the house from himself.

'Not of course that I care,' interjected Mr Smythe hastily.

'You're very broadminded,' said Richard.

'I am,' he said, but then he added, 'I do have a bit of a problem with statues.'

Inevitably, as we moved toward the graveyards of our fourth and final church, the conversation turned to the statue of Our Lady in Ballinspittle, Co. Kerry, which is rumoured to move.

'Why don't all three of us claim we have seen a vision at this spot?' Richard wondered out loud. It would certainly attract pilgrims, we all agreed, to the little lonely country church above us on the hill.

'But what could we sell?' said Mr Smythe, warming to the subject. 'You have to have something to sell. That's the whole point about these miracle places. We can't sell rosary beads, so what could it be?'

'The *Church of Ireland Gazette*, in a booth, here at this gate,' said Richard, following us in, and, as we climbed the little footpath beyond, Mr Smythe's laughter echoed round the yew trees, and his eyes ran, and he wiped his face with his hat.

'My, my, that's a good one,' said Mr Smythe, but Richard had forgotten his quip and was storming ahead.

'This is something special,' he called back to us, and I looked and saw this was so; for a start the sanctuary roof of St Patrick's, Ardagh, was not slated but roofed with limestone flags in the manner of the early Irish Christian churches.

We went inside and found that this tiny estate church, endowed by the Shirley family, had been built to the highest standards. Pews, stained-glass windows, floor tiles with the Shirley arms – every detail was exquisite. There was also that sanctuary roof made from stone. Looking up at it from inside, it resembled a honey-coloured tortoise-back. Unfortunately, though the congregation had recently roofed the rest of the church with asbestos tiles, they had left the sanctuary untouched. Water had consequently poured through on to the altar, and the tiles on the walls were grievously suffering from the damp; many were off and many more soon would be.

'You'll have to repoint the stone roof and probably lead it on the inside,' said Richard to the minister, who had just rejoined us.

'Ah, now,' he said, rubbing his hands. 'They're only after putting the new asbestos roof on it, I don't know whether their funds'll stretch to that.'

'I saw the new roof,' said Richard, who does not share the

modern Irish passion for asbestos, 'and as that wasn't cheap, surely they could afford what I've suggested.'

There was a delicate pause before the rector continued. 'There's only the four families in the congregation, and one of them would not be up to what you're saying, anyway.'

Four families. That was eight adults, at best. It made the twenties and thirties at the other churches suddenly seem enormous.

Sitting in St Patrick's, while Richard paced about, watching the sun streaming through the delicate stained-glass window decorated with grapes and shamrocks, and listening to the wet dripping through the beautiful stone roof over the sanctuary, the Protestant fear – which is every minority's fear, that they are going to disappear – ceased being abstract and became real, for this empty church (and the others before) testified to their decline more visibly than census returns or statistics.

It was nearly four o'clock and getting dark by the time Richard finished, and we went outside. As we said our good-byes, the wind whistled through the Irish yews planted round the church.

'Have you enjoyed yourself?' asked Mr Smythe solicitously.

'Indeed I did.' It was true, I had.

He shook his head.

'You'll have to go out with a clergyman and have a real day some day soon,' he said enigmatically.

Diary

I am reading A.T.Q. Stewart's The Narrow Ground, *subtitled* The Roots of Conflict in Ulster, *an illuminating study of the continuity of political violence, and of the unchanging nature of the conventions which characterized that violence.*

This is a true story Stewart retells, taken from a nineteenth-century work, New Ireland *by A.M. Sullivan. A man called Gorman, the servant of a landlord, is 'out' regularly at night with an underground* tenants' organization, burning property, maiming cattle and terrorizing the Anglo-Saxon landowning invaders.

All goes well for the group, until, one night, they turn up at the house of Gorman's landlord with the intention of killing the master and burning his place down.

Now a different set of rules obtains and – which was common in this situation – loyalty to the 'boys' is superseded by loyalty to the employer. Gorman barricades the premises, and in the ensuing fight mortally wounds one of the chief assailants, a young man whom he knows well and with whom he has been 'out' before.*

*

Shortly after reading this, I am in a county just across the border in the South, staying with some English friends. On Sunday morning my car breaks down, so I borrow my friend H—'s car and drive to the house of the mechanic. When he opens the front door and sees what I have come in, he immediately demands, 'What are you doing with H—'s car?', and it is some minutes before I can convince him I genuinely have the loan of it.

Then I drive the mechanic, his name is J—, to my car in the lane where it has broken down, and he fixes it. Afterwards we have a cigarette together. I tell him where I live, and it turns out J— is from Enniskillen. He tells me where he used to live and work, and he appears to have a native's grasp of the topography.

Then he sighs, and, after drawing on his cigarette, he says, 'But I can't go there any more. No! That's all gone now, that is. Can't go there, I'd be lifted if I did,' and then he adds, 'Et cetera' in order to leave me in no doubt as to what he means. I take this admission of Republican involvement with a pinch of salt and drive him back to his house.

'Sorry I was a bit rough at the start,' he says, and he explains that for a few minutes he thought I had stolen H—'s car (which he knew well, because he had fixed the sump in the garage where he works only

---

* The Narrow Ground: The Roots of Conflict in Ulster, p. 119, quoting from New Ireland, vol. I, pp. 226-7.

the week before) and had seriously considered ringing the Garda and having me arrested.

When I finally get to the house where I am going for lunch, I ask about J——.

'You mean our local Provie,' someone says, and they reel off his record; so many years in the Kesh, so many serious crimes.

'He thought I stole H——'s car. He was going to have me arrested,' I say, simultaneously remembering the story from Sullivan. It isn't an exact comparison, but there's enough common ground for some sort of analogy: 120 years on and the peculiar rules which informed the nineteenth-century agitators still hold. An Englishman might be an enemy if he's a soldier, but if you have fixed his car and you think it's been stolen, you have a duty to call the police.

30

Two Notes

Many images have been applied to the politics and society of Northern Ireland. In my experience shoreline metaphors are the most popular, for these carry within them the idea of something beached, washed-up, stranded, which is probably the general perception of the situation in Northern Ireland, as seen from the rest of the British Isles.

In my salad days I might have subscribed to these metaphors, but now my chosen image would be two trees, old and vast, standing side by side. If we were to delve below the surface of the earth on which they stand, as in a section drawing from one of my childhood encyclopedias, passing through the top soil and the subsequent strata of clay and rock, we would discover that their white roots twist and intertwine to such an extent that it is impossible to sort out which roots belong to which tree.

Back above ground the trees stand apart. They have no ostensible connection, yet they draw nourishment from the same soil, and so bound up are their roots with one another that to pull one tree out would kill the other.

II

In the last twelve months, which has seen the reunification of the two Germanies, many have made an analogy with Ireland. But Ireland is not Germany, and one cannot apply the template of one country to another.

West Germany was rich and East Germany wanted some; here, on the other hand, there is no such economic motor at work.

Diary

An old Fermanagh convention which I have just discovered. Once upon a time, in mixed marriages, all the girls born of the union would follow the religion of their mother, while the boys would follow the religion of their father. Then came Ne Temere *and the tradition vanished.**

---

* Promulgated in 1908, this decree required Catholics in mixed marriages to guarantee before marriage that all children would be raised as Catholics. Those not making the undertaking would not be able to marry in a Catholic church.

31

A Mixed Marriage

I

'I came from Monea originally,' said Millicent, a woman in her forties. We were sitting by the fire in the living-room of her farmhouse.

'We have a rector here called Blythe – he was Church of Ireland – and the Young Farmers' Club had just started, where young people from a farming background could get together, and they offered things like public speaking, debates and so on. And the rector approached people in our area, and he approached people like my husband or the man who was to become my husband, Peter, a Catholic, and asked him if he'd be interested in coming, and Peter said, "Yes." The idea was that it would be interdenominational.

'So we had our first meeting in a school, and it was the first time Protestants and Catholics in my age group got the opportunity to get together. I knew Peter by sight, but in those days you never met people from the Catholic side, and they never met people from our side.

'After that I went away to New Zealand, but I never felt it was my home. That was 1967 to 1971. Then I came back, and I met Peter again, and he invited me out. I was a bit reluctant to go at first because I thought – oh, you know – I'm what I am, and he's what he is. But anyway, he persuaded me, and it became serious. So I went back to New Zealand for another year.

'Anyhow, it didn't work out in New Zealand, for the same reason it hadn't before. So I returned and I started seeing Peter again. My parents at that time spoke to Peter and very tactfully tried to explain what the problems which faced us were, and we discussed them between ourselves. Then we decided we were going to get married. To say people were delighted would be untrue. I don't know if I could go through everything that I went through then. People were dead against it.'

'Why?'

'Because he was a Roman Catholic.'

'Did the fact that if you had children together they would be Roman Catholic affect people's attitudes?'

'Children didn't come into it. We didn't think about them then.'

'Was he having to put up with what you were having to put up with?'

'No, I don't think so. Maybe he was above it. He had that kind of character about him that he didn't worry about these things. You'll have to ask him.'

'And what about the children?'

'I agreed that any children we had would be brought up in his Church.'

'Why?'

'I was coming to live here in Peter's home with his parents and so on, and I thought it would be very hard for them if I was to come in here and then announce that our children were going to be brought up in my Church. I thought it would be much better if I just said that our children were going to be brought up in their Church. Maybe I was soft, I don't know.'

II

'Where were you married?'

'In Peter's church. Sounds very much like a one-way street here, doesn't it? We married in his church, yes. And I found that my minister didn't support me. At the time, that is.

When I went to him before we got married, he said, "You'll be ostracized!" That was all.'

'Was it a church wedding?'

'Yes.'

'Did your parents attend?'

'No, they refused to come, yet they weren't hostile – especially my mother. Now my father didn't like it – he was a member of the Orange Order – and he made no bones about it, he wasn't happy.'

'What about the rest of your family?'

'Only one sister and one brother came. The rest of them – we were a very big family – they didn't.'

'Didn't you feel lonely without your parents there?'

'No, I'd made the decision. This was what I was going to do, and so I went ahead and did it.'

III

'We didn't have a honeymoon, because I had only a week off work. What we decided we'd do instead was that we would go and visit all the members of my family and bring them each a piece of wedding cake. These were all the members of my family who hadn't come to the wedding, you see.

'So we called on each of them, one after the other, and there was no real warmth coming from any of them. But I didn't pay any attention to this, and I would say to them, "Come up and see the wedding presents," and they would come and that was a good thing because then they saw Peter didn't have two heads.

'Relations were completely restored, I would say, by the time my first child Martha was born. I remember very clearly how pleased my father was to see me after the wedding, and he was not a man who showed his feelings.'

'Did you talk to your parents about the wedding which they hadn't been to?'

'Of course I did. I wasn't going to pretend it hadn't happened. I showed them the wedding pictures and everything. This was something I was going to do at all costs, and no one was going to stop me.'

'What did you feel when the children were born and they started going to Peter's church?'

'I couldn't see much wrong in Peter's church, and if what I saw in him was in his church, it was all right by me.'

IV

'This whole thing – and I've been married now eighteen years – has been an education. My family have got to meet people like the priest, whom they would never have met before. And now we've come to the stage that they don't care if the priest comes into the house a lot. This is how things have changed. Before you never had any way of knowing the other side, but since I've done this we have, or they have, and that can only be a good thing. I think you miss out a lot if you don't meet the people from the other side of the house.'

*

After the conversation I met Millicent's first daughter, Martha. A Catholic, her intention is to join the RUC and make her career there.

Diary

The seventeen-year-old son of a friend comes home, ashen faced and upset. Some of his friends, he explains, have gone into the UDA, and he has agreed to follow them. He is to meet a UDA organizer to complete his induction later in the day. But he has made a terrible mistake, he admits, and he doesn't want to join. Only he can't see how to get out of it without incurring the same fate as X, who, having agreed to join, then failed to show up to make his pledge. 'They held him down in a field and ran over his legs with a tractor,' he tells them.

'If you join now,' his father says, 'they are going to have their claws into you for the rest of your life.'

His son doesn't join, and a couple of days later he leaves for England.

32

My Last Parade

By chance, a year on, I was once again in Scotland the day before the Twelfth of July – this time not at the port of Stranraer but at Glasgow Airport.

In the departure lounge, very early in the morning, the only other passenger was a woman in her fifties. Her hair was the colour of straw. She wore a leather skirt, which is not what one identifies with a typical Orange matron.

After a few moments she jumped up from the bucket seat she was sitting on. She turned and stared out of the window. She bit into the hard skin at the side of her thumbnail. She sat down. She jumped up again.

'Aeroplanes aren't so bad,' I said, or something like that.

'I know that.' There was a slight tetchiness in her voice. 'I've just flown from Canada.' Her accent was a mixture of Ulster and North American.

'Is something the matter?'

It all tumbled out. She played with an Orange band from Vancouver who were already in Northern Ireland. She was joining them. They were going to march the next day, the tercentenary of the Battle of the Boyne, and she was terrified by what she had seen on television. She had not been 'home' since her parents took her to Canada as a child in the 1950s.

'You'll be fine,' I said.

'How do you know?'

'On the Twelfth they wouldn't dare attack a parade.'

This attempt to smooth anxieties by seeming to be an expert completely backfired.

'How do you know?' she demanded. Her face whitened. Her eyes widened. She wrung her hands. Because I had said nothing would happen, I had implied that it could – otherwise why would I have bothered to speak?

'We're going to Enniskillen,' she said. 'There was a big bombing there, wasn't there?'

'That's where I live. A lovely place.'

The conversation ended. She went back to pacing up and down, gnawing at her fingers and twisting her face. I looked through the windows and felt sorry anyone should feel as frightened as she did, especially about a place which I now knew. The runway outside was covered with a fine dew, and every time a vehicle passed two lines appeared after the tyres in the wet.

At the door the detective on duty stopped a bandy-legged man with a broken nose and a plastic carrier-bag filled with cans of Tennant's lager.

'ID?'

'Sorry, pal.'

'You must have some sort of identification.'

Bandy pulled one of his pockets inside out to show it was empty. 'Sorry, pal. Nothing doing.'

It was the same tale, over and over again with the Orangemen who followed him. They carried nothing except their drink and their certainty. They were travelling within their own country. Why did they need proof of who they were?

12 JULY

The next day, in Enniskillen, when I went to see the marching by the Orange Lodges and the bands, I was on the look-out for the woman from the airport. I met her as she and her band were coming down from the field and starting to march back towards the main street. She wore a blue jacket and a peaked hat. She played the tuba.

I waved and called out, 'Hello.' She did not return the greeting. I thought this was strange. Band members and Orangemen always responded to friends in the watching crowds. It was part of the etiquette of the occasion.

I wondered if she did not recognize me. However, then, watching her marching away, I noticed her posture was twisted and defensive. She had not seen me, I decided, because she was not seeing anything. She was just getting through the ordeal.

I wandered up to the High Street. The first part of the day, which I had spent up here watching the bands and the Orange Lodges parading with their banners out towards the field, had been exciting and stirring, with the crowds cheering and the music swirling around.

On returning, however, I noticed a change in the atmosphere. The crowds along the pavements were thinner. Those who had left were mainly the families. Those who remained were mainly the young, full of bravura and drink as they shouted and jostled.

I found a space on the kerb. On the other side of the road a girl suddenly ran out with a camera. I looked to see what it was she wanted to photograph. It was a band. At the front there were three pretty girls parading party colours – blue and orange flags. They were followed by a line of drummers, some in dark glasses. There were ten or twelve, and they were sweeping forward with military precision while beating savagely down with their sticks.

The bands, which now passed, were all playing faster and harder than they had on the way up. Their energy was clearly raising the adrenalin level in the crowds, and the crowds with their cheering and shouting were clearly lifting the adrenalin level of the bands.

I did not feel comfortable. If the earlier part of the day had been Dr Jekyll, this was now Mr Hyde. No longer was the parade something from folk culture which, in the true sense, was family entertainment. It had reverted to being the celebration of a victory in a civil war, as is every Irish parade, Green as well as Orange. It had become hard, tough and potentially violent.

Nowhere was this more evident than with the Lambeg and big-drum players. On the way up they had cavorted and writhed. They had been figures of fun straight from carnival, cartoon exhibitionists – and the crowds loved them. But now, on the way down, they flailed their sticks in a frenzy, as if possessed, oblivious of their bleeding knuckles and their burst blisters.

Behind me some youths spilled out of a pub and began to scrap in a half amiable, half hostile sort of way.

It was time to leave.

Diary

Something from my diary of 1989.

On Any Questions today, BBC Radio 4, one question is, 'Should the UDR be disbanded?'

The panel are John Prescott, Angela Rumbold, Sara Parkin of the Greens and the vice-chairman of the Liberal Democrats. [I forget his name – I've lost that bit of paper.]

They all have absolutely nothing to say except that the force cannot be prejudged on the strength of a few rotten apples.

In addition John Prescott admits to finding the Northern Ireland problem very depressing.

Sara Parkin suspects UDR misbehaviour upsets the Nationalists.

They say nothing that hasn't been said before: it is very disappointing.

*

It is now a year on since I wrote the above. It is a couple of days after the Twelfth.

Catholic friends to dinner last night. The business of UDR leakage to Protestant paramilitaries comes up in conversation.

'Christ,' says one of my friends, 'if I was in the UDR and I got an IRA man or a Sinn Féin sympathizer at a checkpoint, I'd beat the shit out of him. The law can't touch those ones. The security services have to take it into their own hands sometimes.'

It is not so important that it is a Catholic who is speaking, as that it is the idea of illicit retribution that is being supported. This is the moment when the paramilitaries have succeeded.

*

The very last day of research. I explore the old Catholic graveyard in Enniskillen. It is walled, and inside the gate I find the very first grave belongs to one Thomas Smollen (1829–1909), parish priest of Enniskillen in the last century. I have Livingstone's The Fermanagh Story with me, but Smollen, which sounds so Protestant, is not listed in the section 'British Families of Fermanagh'. I have better luck, however, with some of the other unlikely names in the graveyard, which include Carson, Johnston, Sommerville and Thompson. All were English, yet here they are, sandwiched between Corrigans, Dohertys, Gallaghers and of course Maguires, all of them obviously having at some point converted.

On the far side of the graveyard I look across the river to Enniskillen. It is a good place to get a sense of the town as an island. It is also a good place to consider the myth that here there are two monolithic communities, Protestant and Catholic, and that they have stared angrily at each other down the centuries. The evidence of the graveyard disproves that. Enniskillen – until comparatively recent times anyway – was an island town, and on such places people intermingle. That was how one got Catholic and Protestant Carsons.

Epilogue

I

In the *Impartial Reporter* I read that at a press conference in Stormont, the education minister for Northern Ireland, Dr Brian Mawhinney, announced 100 per cent grant aid for the Enniskillen integrated school. In other words, the school has now been recognized by the government as fulfilling a need, and in future the financial burden will be shouldered by the state instead of by parents.

II

Richard Pierce telephones and tells me the design for the addition to Enniskillen war memorial ('Gaudi's doves', he refers to it in shorthand) has been accepted by the committee charged with overseeing the project; but his wording 'In memory of our neighbours . . .' has not. Apparently some relatives feel that something like 'Murdered by terrorists', for instance, would be more accurate. There will have to be a compromise.*

'Ah, well,' he says sanguinely, 'there was a time when they would have let an architect like Michelangelo do the words as well, but that was then and this is now.'

---

* It was finally agreed that the inscription should read, 'In remembrance of 11 of our neighbours who were killed by a terrorist bomb at this site on Remembrance Sunday 8th November 1987.'

From a letter to a friend:

Dear —

Here is a summary (intended to give you a flavour but not the detail) of my search for the cook – the Catholic one I hoped to prove was making Brookeborough's dinners at the time he was declaring he didn't employ Catholics.

At the start I thought I was looking for a McKeagney. Then the woman's name changed to Hoey. Then that line fouled up, because at the time my Catholic was possibly working in Colebrooke in the kitchens, there was also a Protestant Hoey – the wife of the land steward Hoey – and she *also* worked in the kitchens. And if that wasn't complicated enough, my Hoey then metamorphosed via marriage into a Monaghan, and later, after Mr Monaghan died, changed again into a Carlin. It was when I realized I was going to have to go trawling through all the records after four names that I lost my patience with this genealogical quest and abandoned it.

However, shortly after this, I was put in touch with a man who had been chauffeur at Colebrooke from the early twenties to 1941. He definitely confirmed that there were no Catholics working in the house in his time – which made me feel good about having abandoned my quest. He also thought there had been a Catholic cook later on, and that Monaghan might well have been her name (which made sense).

'So there weren't any Catholics there?'

'In the house, no!' he said breezily. 'On the other hand, there was as many working on the estate as Protestants.'

'Even in 1933?'

'Didn't I say so?'

And now, out of the blue, it seems you have turned up those pages from the Colebrooke cash book, which you say, judging by the names, confirms what the chauffeur said.*

So it seems the little story I've been chasing after – that Brookeborough delivered his speeches and then came home to a dinner prepared by a Catholic cook – is not to be. I'm sad it didn't come off, because if it had, it would have said something about this place and the intermingling that goes on in a way that would have been neat and satisfying and literary. But there *is* the cash book. So what the story of the cook represented was true, is true – of course he had Catholics about the place, when he said he didn't have any – only the proof, those photocopied pages you're forwarding, they do not have quite the same magic as the cook. Life is never as good as it is in stories, but then it wouldn't be life if it was, would it?

* Public Records Office, Northern Ireland, Brookeborough Papers, D998/3/21. Page 134 of the cash book had almost nothing but Catholic names on it. It is dated January 1934, but it refers to payment for work done the previous year, which was when most of the 'notorious' speeches were made.

List of Sources

Barton, Brian, *Brookeborough: The Making of a Prime Minister* (Belfast, 1988)

Churchill, Sir Winston, *The World Crisis. Vol. IV: The Aftermath* (London, 1929)

Curran, P.S, 'Psychiatric Aspects of Terrorist Violence: Northern Ireland 1969–1987', *British Journal of Psychiatry* (1988), no. 153.

Fisk, Robert, *In Time of War: Ireland, Ulster and the Price of Neutrality 1939–1945* (London, 1983)

Flackes, W.D. and Elliott, Sydney, *Northern Ireland: A Political Directory 1968–1988* (Belfast, 1989)

Foster, R.F., *Modern Ireland 1600–1972* (London, 1988)

Leonard, Jane, 'War Memorials' in *Ireland and the First World War*, ed. David Fitzpatrick (Dublin, 1986)

Livingstone, Peadar, *The Fermanagh Story* (Enniskillen, 1969)

Murphy, Dervla, *A Place Apart* (London, 1978)

Rowan, Alistair, *North West Ulster* (London, 1979)

Stewart, A.T.Q., *The Narrow Ground: The Roots of Conflict in Ulster* (London, 1977)

Thackeray, William Makepeace, *The Irish Sketch-Book 1843* (Stroud, 1990 edition)

Tóibín, Colm, *Walking along the Border* (London, 1987)

Vargas Llosa, Mario, *Who Killed Palomino Molero?* (London, 1989)

Abacus now offers an exciting range of quality titles by both established and new authors. All of the books in this series are available from:
  Little, Brown and Company (UK) Limited,
  Cash Sales Department,
  P.O. Box 11,
  Falmouth,
  Cornwall TR10 9EN.

Alternatively you may fax your order to the above address. Fax No. 0326 376423.

Payments can be made as follows: Cheque, postal order (payable to Little, Brown and Company) or by credit cards, Visa/Access. Do not send cash or currency. UK customers and B.F.P.O.: please send a cheque or postal order (no currency) and allow £1.00 for postage and packing for the first book, plus 50p for the second book, plus 30p for each additional book up to a maximum charge of £3.00 (7 books plus).

Overseas customers including Ireland, please allow £2.00 for postage and packing for the first book, plus £1.00 for the second book, plus 50p for each additional book.

NAME (Block Letters) ....

ADDRESS...

....

☐ I enclose my remittance for _____

☐ I wish to pay by Access/Visa Card

Number ☐☐☐☐☐☐☐☐☐☐☐☐☐☐☐☐

Card Expiry Date ☐☐☐☐